T-Splines in Autodesk Fusion 360: A Beginners Guide

Tutorial Books

Contents

T-Splines in Autodesk Fusion 360: A Beginner's Guide

The T-Spline tools allows you to create organic smooth solid or surface models by manipulating and subdividing the primitive shapes such as spheres, blocks, cylinders, and so on. These tools are available on the **Form** toolbar.

Activating the Form toolbar

On the toolbar, click **Solid** tab > **Create** panel > **Create Form** to activate the Form toolbar. The tools available on the **Form** toolbar are shown in the below figure.

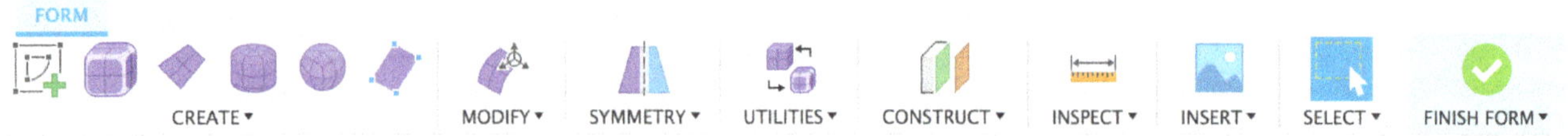

Creating Primitive Shapes

In the **Form** environment, first, you create primitive shapes and then refine them into finished models. The primitive shapes are simple geometric models such as a sphere, cylinder, box, and torus. They are completely airtight closed surfaces. The commands on the **Create** panel help you to create different primitive shapes. The procedures to create different primitive shapes are explained next.

Creating a Quadball

To create a quad ball, activate the **Quadball** command (on the toolbar, click **Form > Create > Quadball**). Next, select a plane from the graphics window. Specify the origin point of the quadball; the quadball is displayed in the graphics window. Click and drag the arrow displayed on the quadball to change its size (or) type-in a value in the **Diameter** box displayed on the quadball.

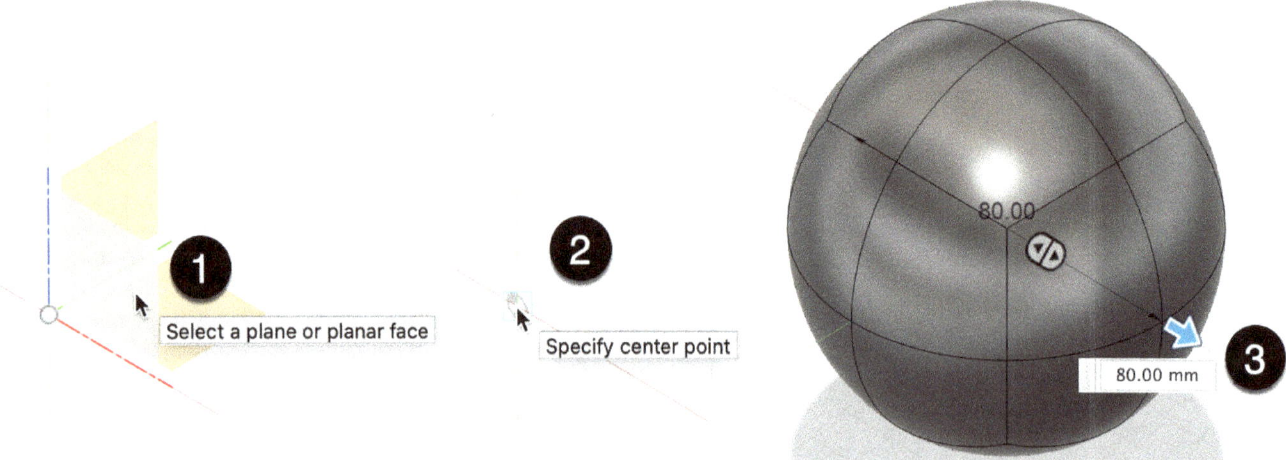

Next, you need to define the number of segments by entering a value in the **Span Faces** box. The **1** value creates a sphere with six segments. The **4** value creates a ninety-six segmented sphere. Likewise, increase the Span Faces value to create a sphere with more segments.

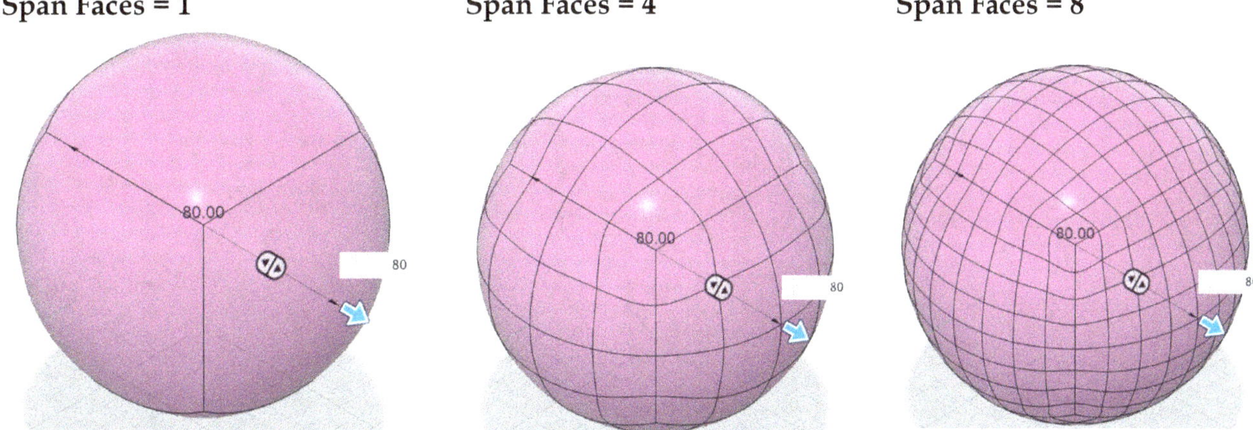

Select the **None** or **Mirror** option from the **Symmetry** drop-down. The **Mirror** option creates symmetry in any of the three directions. To make the length of the quadball symmetrical about the midplane, select **Length Symmetry**. To make the height symmetrical, choose **Height Symmetry**. To make the width symmetrical, select **Width Symmetry**. Click **OK** to generate the quadball.

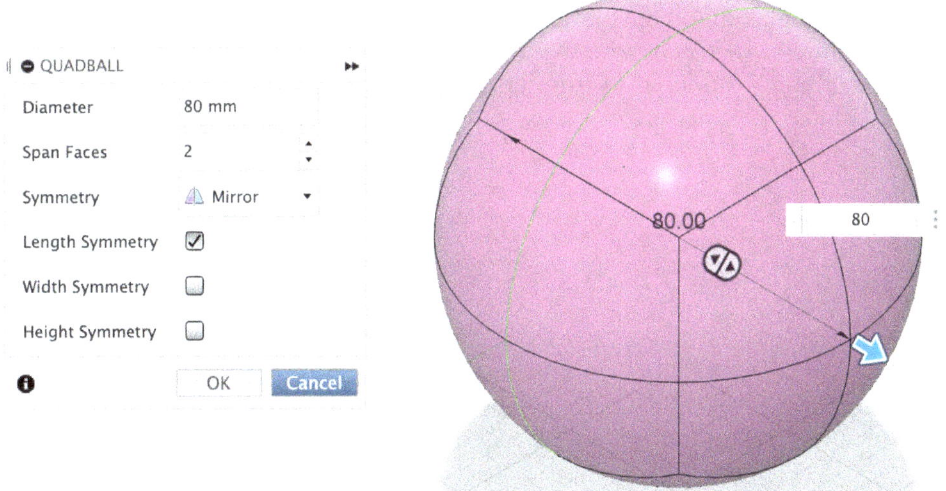

Creating a Sphere

This command creates T-spline sphere. The sphere has faces divided along the latitude and longitudinal directions. Whereas, the quad ball has faces divided along the four directions. Activate this command (click **Form > Create > Sphere** on the toolbar) and select a reference plane. Next, specify the center point of the sphere; the **Sphere** dialog appears. On this dialog, specify the **Diameter**, **Longitude Faces** and **Latitude Faces** values. You can also specify these values by dragging the handles displayed on the sphere. Next, specify the **Symmetry** option and click **OK**.

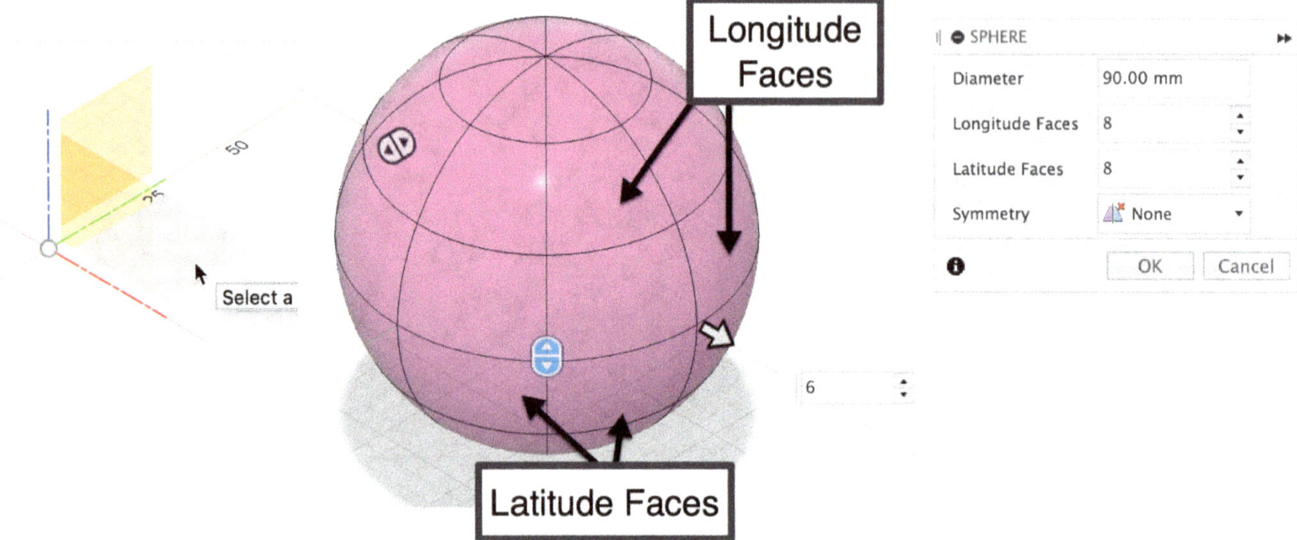

Creating a Cylinder

To create a cylinder, activate the **Cylinder** command (on the toolbar, click **Form > Create > Cylinder**). Select the placement plane from the graphics window. Specify the origin point of the cylinder. Move the pointer outward and click to specify the diameter of the cylinder; the **Cylinder** dialog appears.

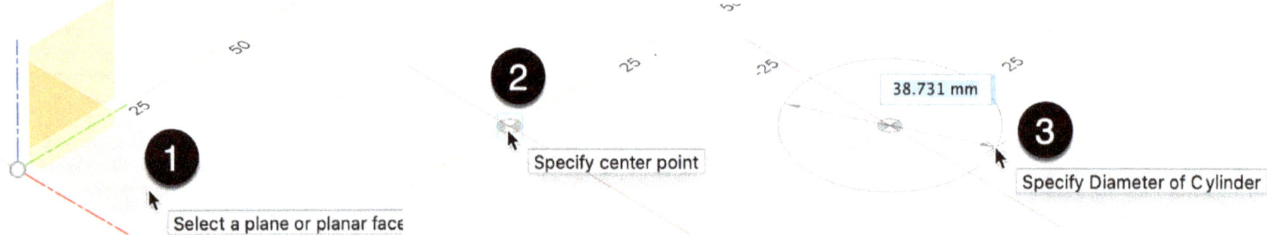

Type in values in the **Diameter** and **Height** boxes on the **Cylinder** dialog. Next, specify the number of segments in the linear and circular direction by entering values in the **Height Faces** and **Diameter Faces** boxes available on the **Cylinder** dialog.

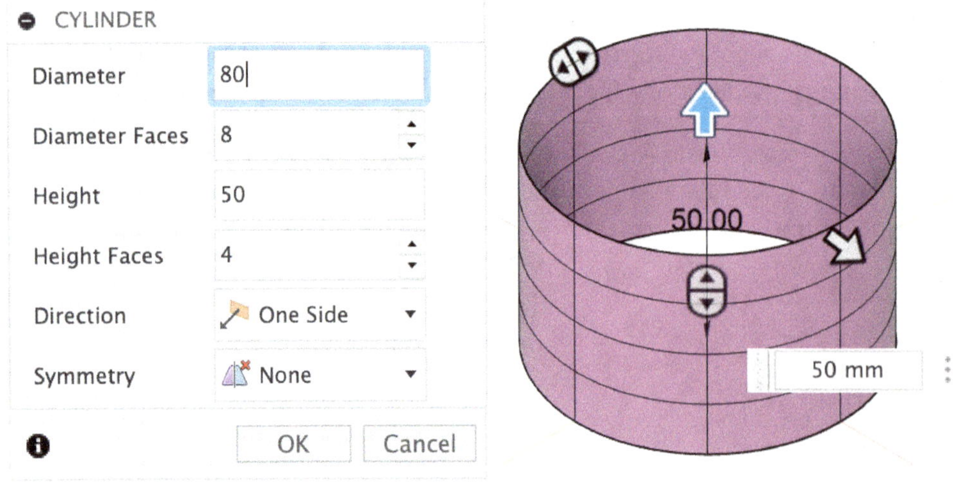

Height Faces: 3
Diameter Faces: 4

Height Faces: 4
Diameter Faces: 6

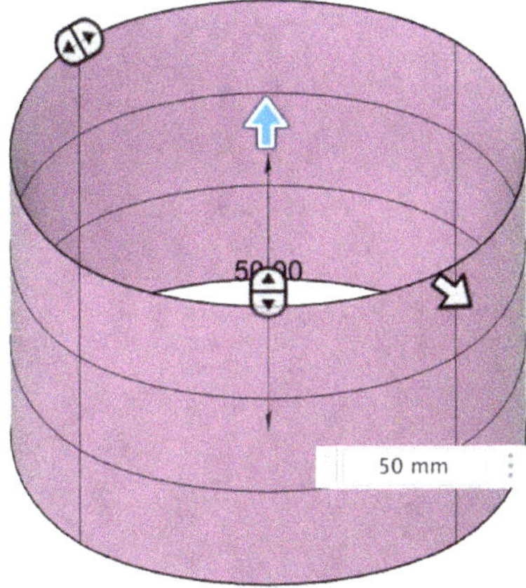

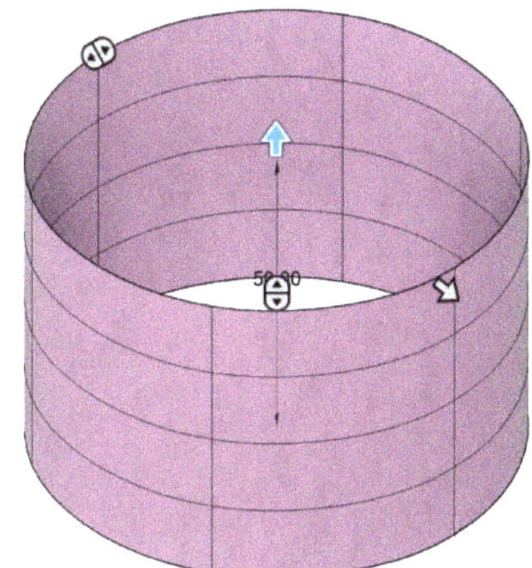

Select the **Mirror** or **Circular** option from the **Symmetry** drop-down. The **Mirror** option creates symmetry in any of the three directions. To make the length of the cylinder symmetrical about the midplane, select **Length Symmetry**. To make the height symmetrical, choose **Height Symmetry**. To make the width symmetrical, select **Width Symmetry**.

Length Symmetry

Width Symmetry

Height Symmetry

The **Circular** option patterns the lateral faces of the cylinder in a circular fashion. For example, create a cylinder and type **3** in the **Diameter Faces** box. Next, select **Symmetry > Circular** and type **2** in the **Symmetric Faces** box; the diameter faces are patterned in the circular fashion two times. It results in six diameter faces. Click **OK** to create cylinder.

Creating a Box

To create a box, activate the **Box** command (on the toolbar, click **Form > Create > Box**). Next, specify the box's location and size using any one of the options available in the **Rectangle** drop-down.

Center

Select this option from the **Rectangle** drop-down. Next, click on the XZ Plane to specify the location of the box. Next, specify the center of the rectangle. Move the pointer outward and click (or) enter the length, width, and angle values in the value boxes displayed in the graphics window.

Specify the height of the box by entering a value in the **Height** box or dragging the arrow displayed in the perpendicular direction of the sketch.

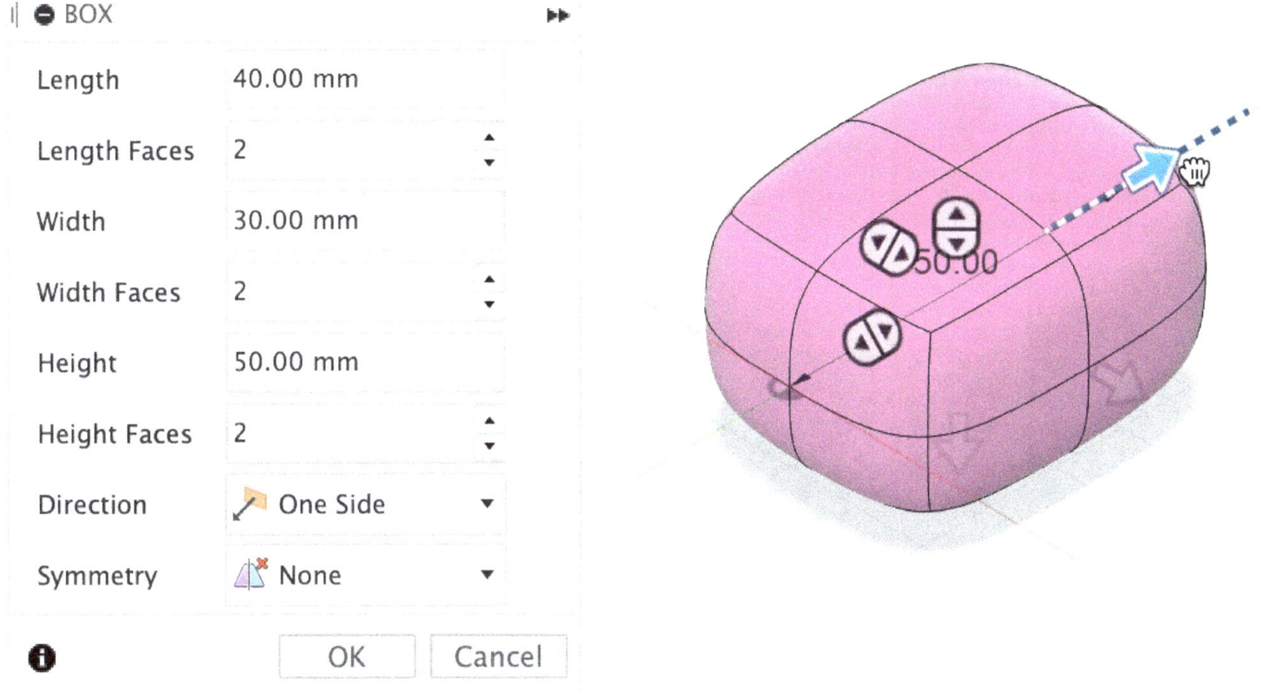

By 2 Points

Activate the Box command and select this option from the **Rectangle** drop-down. Next, click on the XZ plane to specify the first corner rectangle. Move the pointer diagonally and click to specify the second corner of the rectangle. Next, drag the arrow displayed in the perpendicular direction of the sketch.

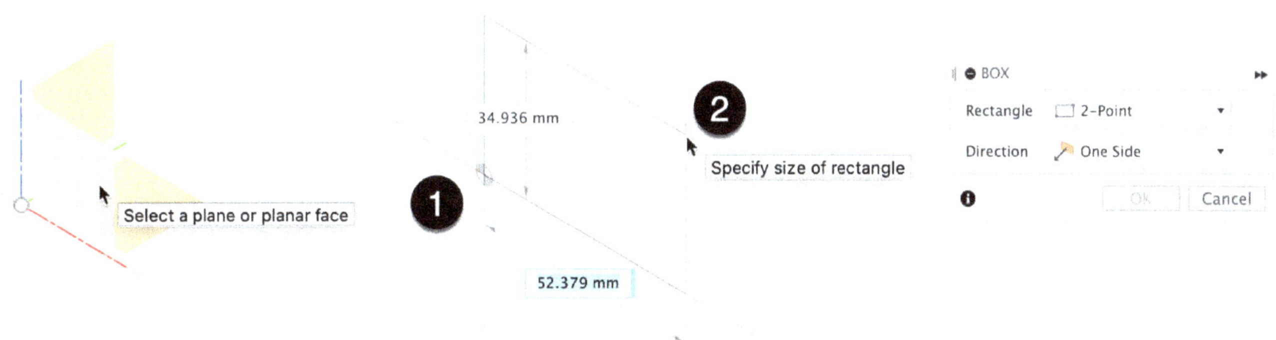

Next, type-in values in the **Length Face**, **Width Faces**, and **Height Faces** boxes to add faces along the length, width, and height of the box, respectively. Click **OK** to complete the box.

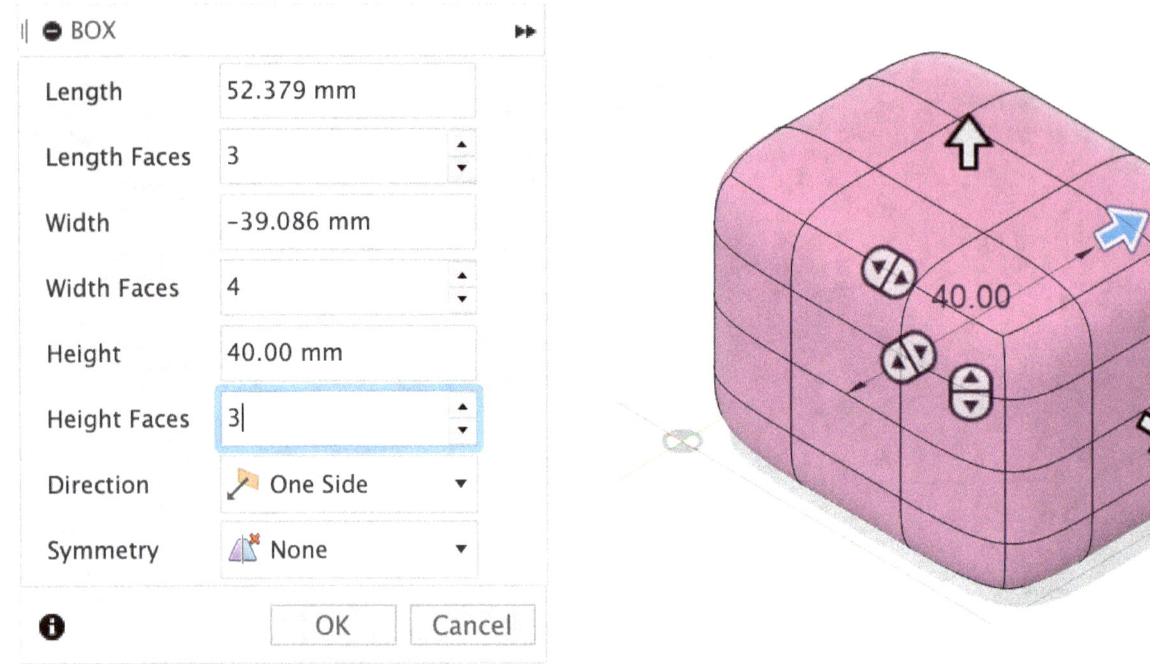

Creating a Torus

To create a torus, activate the **Torus** command (on the toolbar, click **Form > Create > Torus**). Next, select a place on which the torus will be created. Specify the center point of the torus, move the pointer outward and click. Next, enter values in the **Diameter 1** and **Diameter 2** boxes.

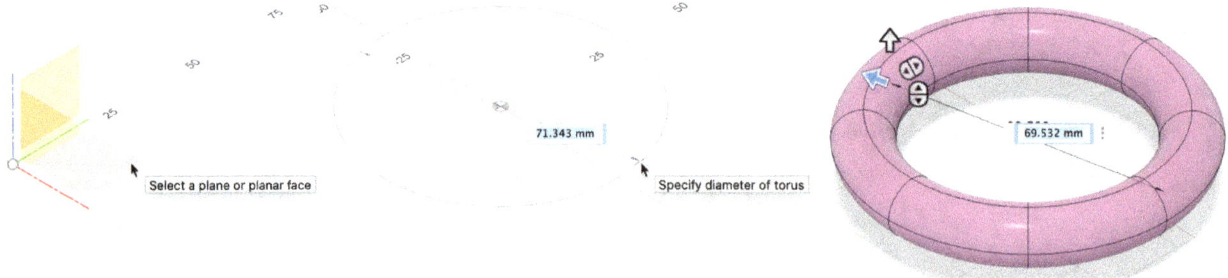

Next, specify the number of segments in the radial and circular direction by entering values in the **Diameter 1 Faces** and **Diameter 2 Faces** boxes. Click **OK** to create the torus.

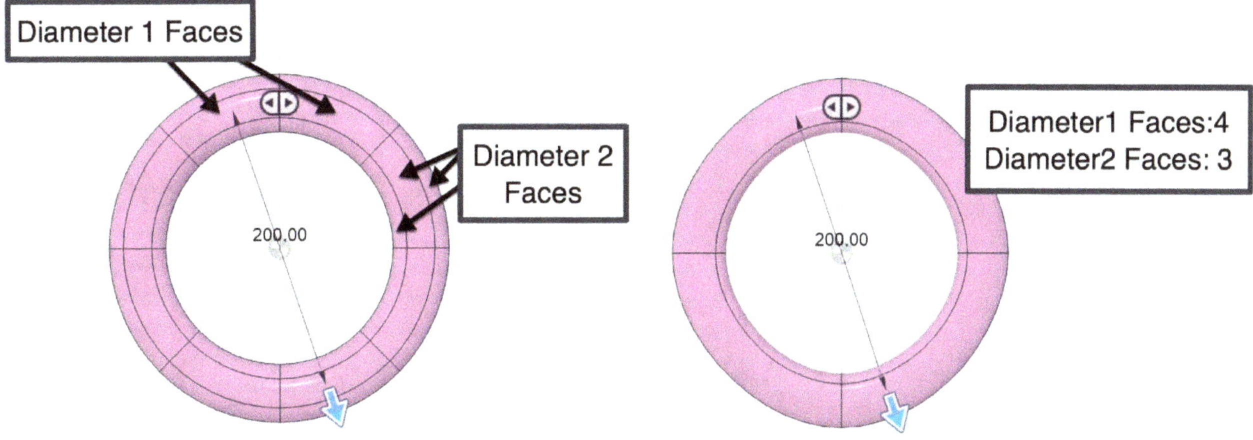

Creating a Plane

To create a plane, click **Form > Create > Plane** on the toolbar, and then select a reference plane. Next, select an option from the **Rectangle** drop-down. For example, select the **Center** option and specify the center point of the rectangle. Move the pointer and click to specify the corner or the rectangle. On the **Plane** dialog, type in values in the **Length** and **Width** boxes to specify the size of the plane. Next, type-in values in the **Length Faces** and **Width Faces** boxes to divide the plane into a number of segments along the length and width of the plane.

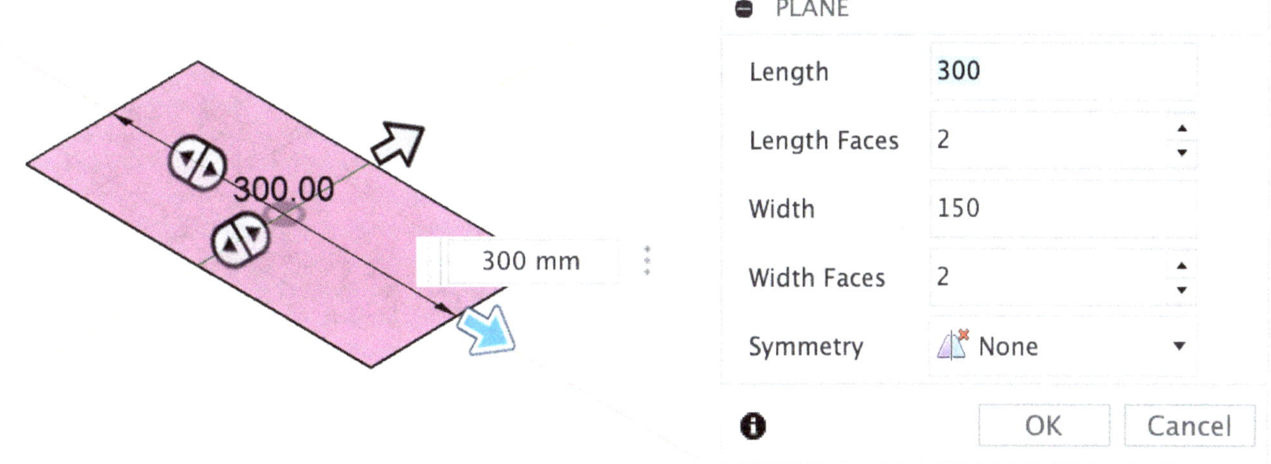

Face

This command creates T-spline by using four or more points that you specify. Activate this command (click **Form**

> Create > Face on the toolbar) and select a reference plane. Next, select **Number of Sides > Rectangle** from the **Face** dialog. Select four points from the . Click **OK** to create the four point surface.

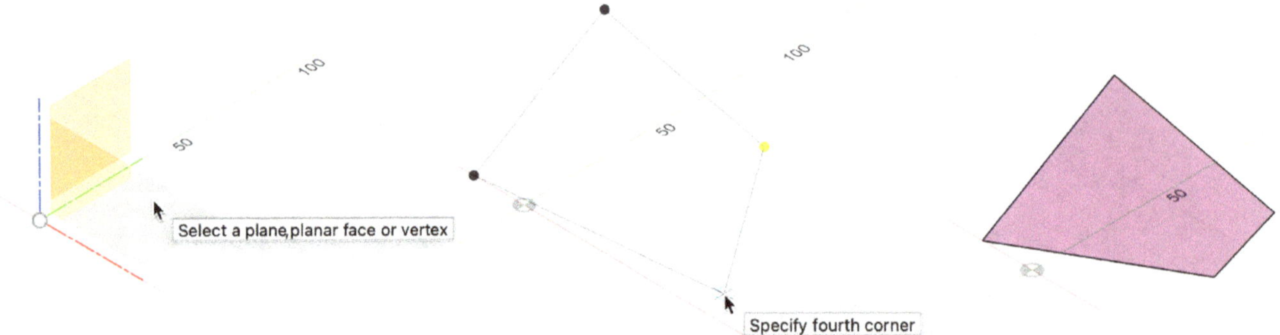

You can also close the opening of a T-spline geometry using the **Face** command. To do this, activate the **Face** command and select **Number of Sides > Multiple Sides** on the **Face** dialog. Next, select **Mode > Simple** . Select the corner points of the opening, as shown. Again, select the first corner point; a face is created closing the opening. Click **OK** on the **Face** dialog.

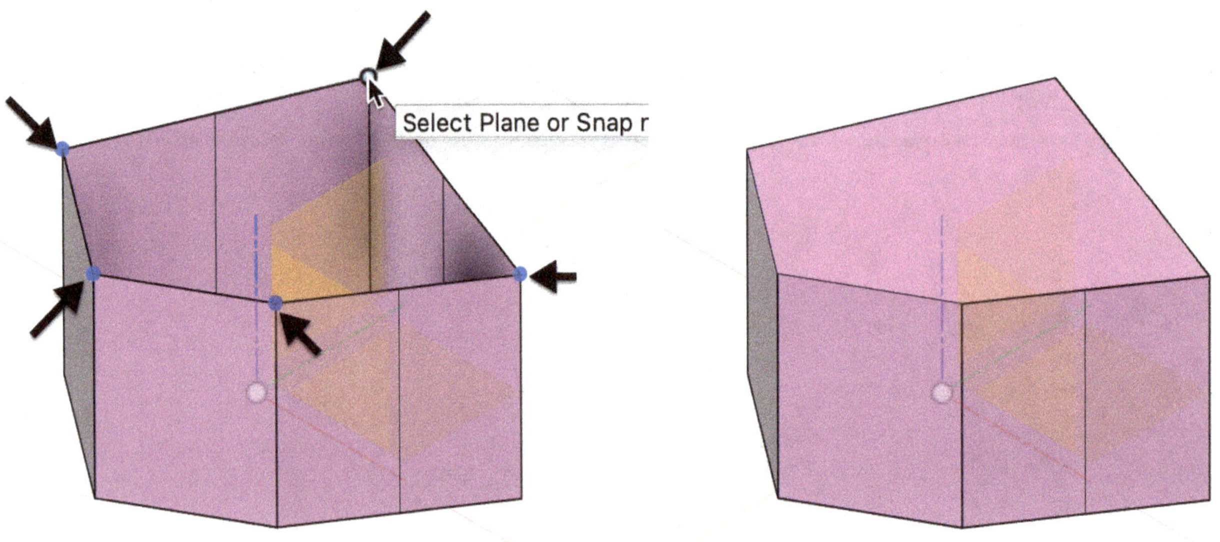

Select **Mode > Edge** and then select and edge of the opening; the vertices of the selected edge are selected. Next, select two vertices from the opening; a four sided face is created.

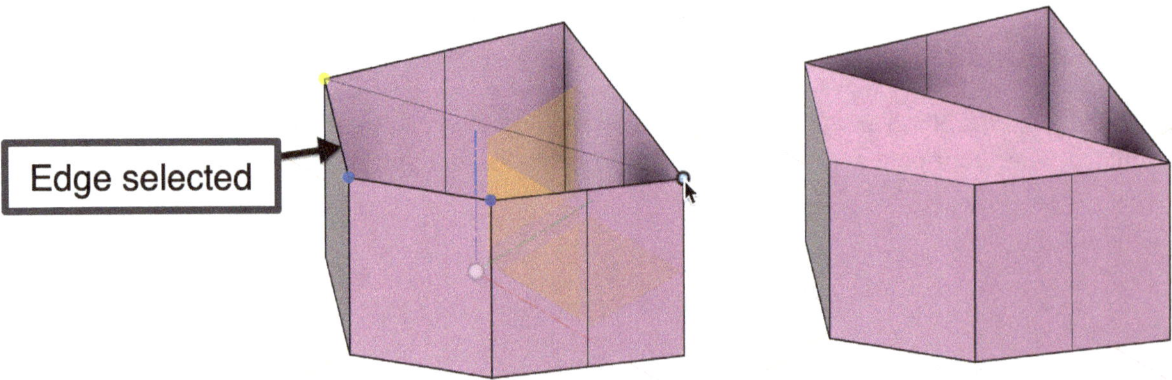

Select **Mode > Chain** and then select and edge of the opening; the vertices of the selected edge are selected. Next, select two vertices from the opening; a four sided face is created. Select another vertex; a face is added connecting the previous face. Click **OK** to complete the face creation.

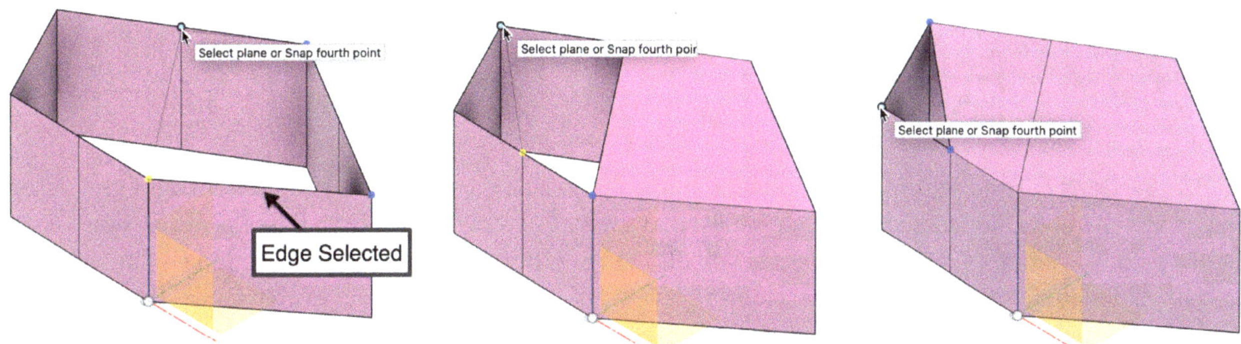

The Pipe command

The **Pipe** command creates a T-spline pipe using a sketch as its path. Activate this command

(on the toolbar, click **Form > Create > Pipe**), and click on a line or curve. On the **Pipe** dialog, click the **Sections** tab and enter a value in the **Global Diameter** box. Next, specify the Display Mode. You can select the

Box Display or **Smooth Display** option.

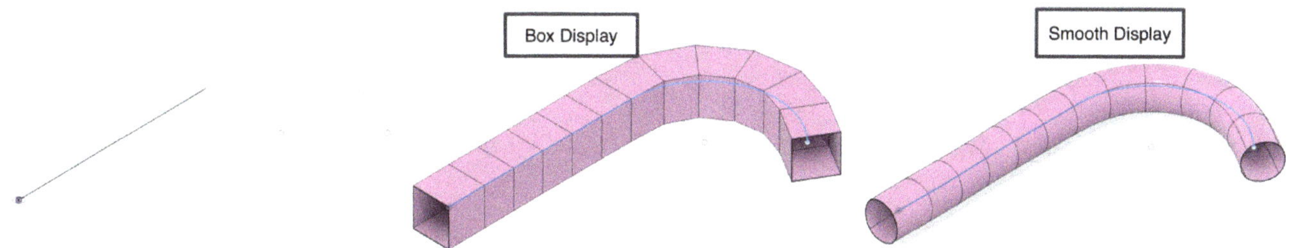

Click the **End Types** tab and select an option from the **End Type** drop-down. There are three options in this drop-down: **Open**, **Square**, and **Spike**. The **Open** option keeps the pipe ends open. The **Square** option closes the pipe ends with a square face. The **Spike** option closes the pipe ends with spikes.

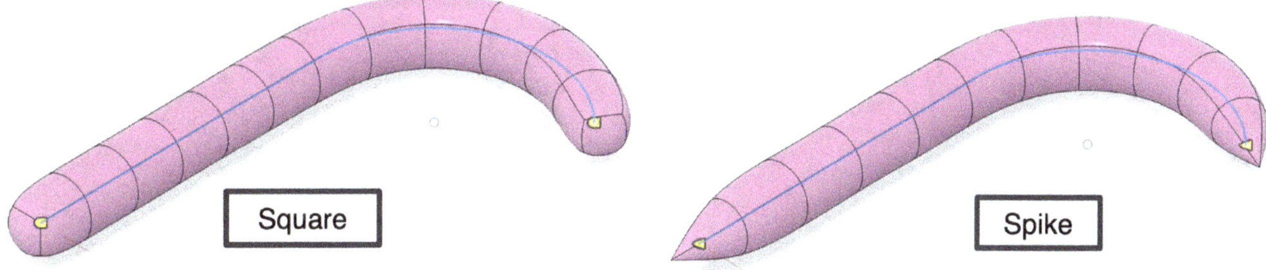

Click the **Segments** tab and use the **Density** slider to specify the segments along the pipe.

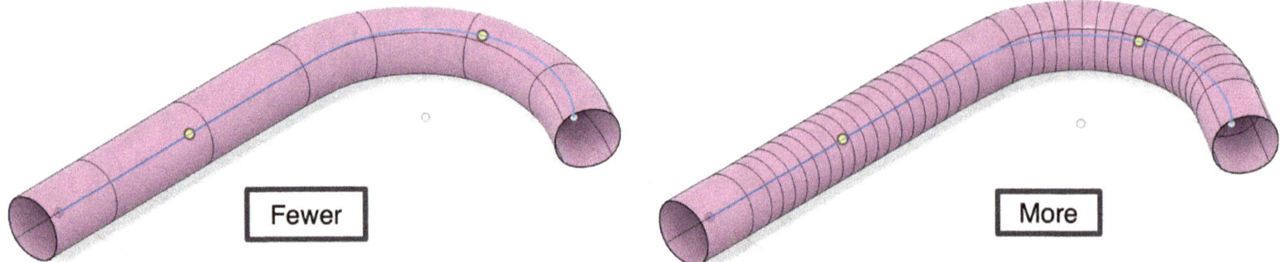

Click the **Sections** tab and select the **Section** button; the sections of the pipe are highlighted in light grey color. Click on anyone of the sections highlighted; notice that the arrows are displayed on the selected section. Click and drag the arrow pointing in the direction perpendicular to the pipe; the diameter of the section is changed. You can also change the diameter of the section by entering a value in the **Diameter** box available on the **Pipe** dialog. Click and drag the arrow displayed along the pipe; the position of the section is changed. You can also enter a value in the **Position** box.

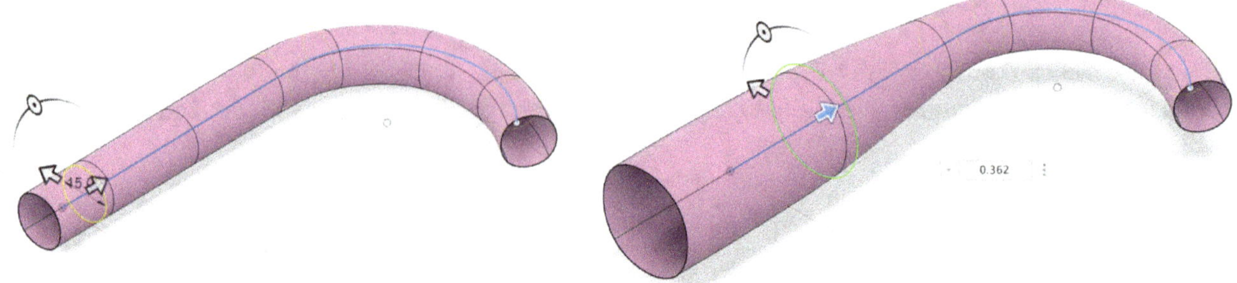

On the **Pipe** dialog, select **Display Mode > Box Display**. Next, change the value in the **Angle** box and notice that the pipe is twisted at the selected section point.

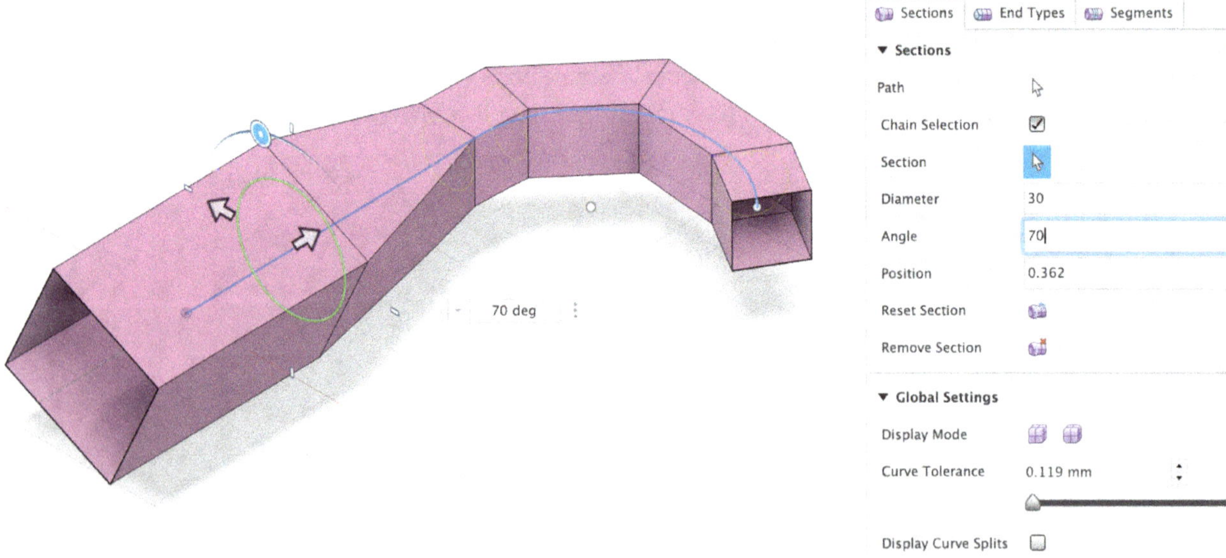

The Extrude command

The **Extrude** command is used to extrude the sketches and faces of the T-splines. For example, create a sketch on anyone of the reference planes. Next, activate the **Extrude** command (on the toolbar, click **From > Create > Extrude**) and click on the sketch. Click an drag the arrow displayed on the selected sketch; the extrusion distance is specified. Click and drag the Angle handle to taper the extrusion. You can also specify the taper angle in the **Angle** box available on the **Extrude** dialog.

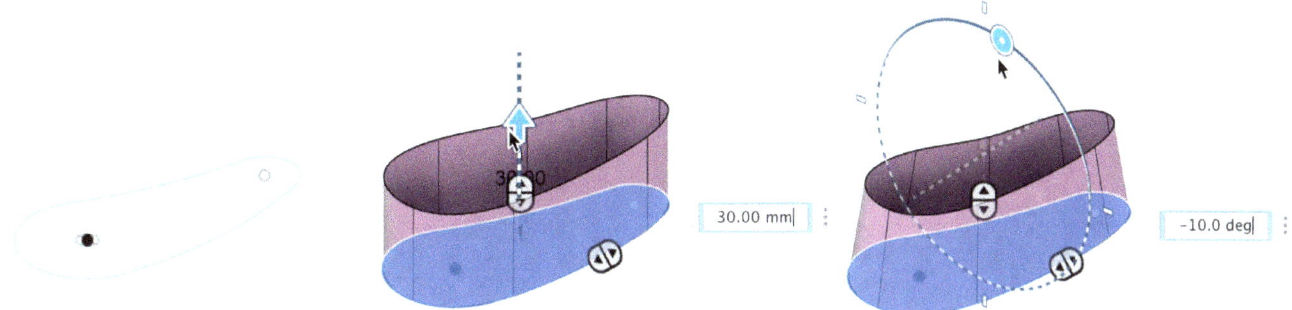

The extrusion is divided into different faces. You can specify the number of faces in the **Faces** box. You can define the spacing of the faces using two methods available in the **Spacing** drop-down. The **Curvature** option defines the spacing of the faces based on the curvature of the extruded T-spline surface. The **Uniform** option divides the extrusion into uniform faces irrespective of the curvature.

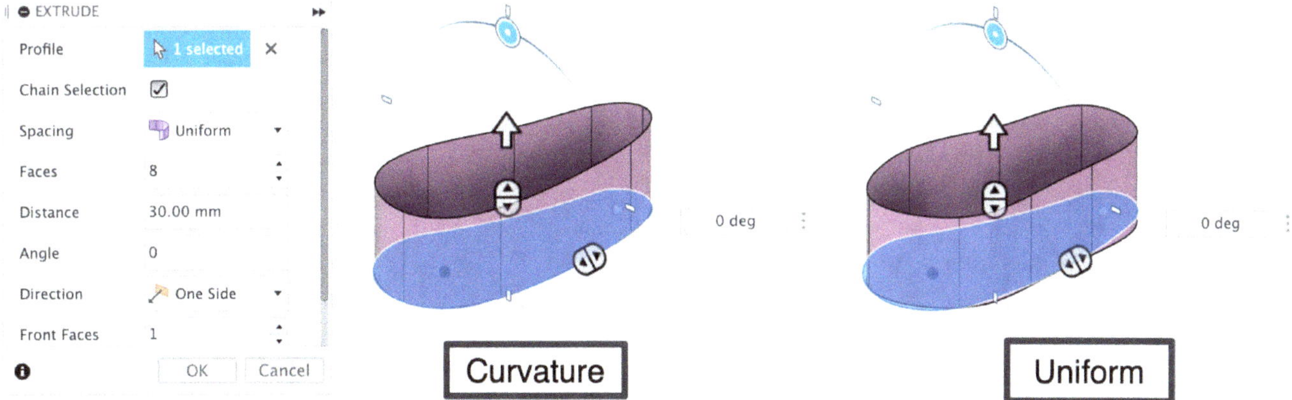

You can also add faces in the direction perpendicular to the selected face or sketch. To do this, type-in a value in the **Front Faces** box. You can also drag the handle displayed on the extrusion to specify the front faces.

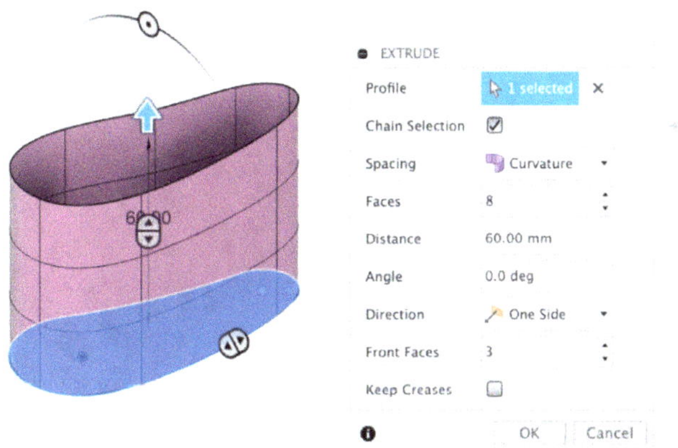

Extruding the Faces of a T-Spline Surface

This command is practically illustrated in the following example. First, create a box using the Box command, as shown. Next, activate the Extrude command (on the toolbar, click Form > Create > Extrude) and click on the upper side faces, as shown. Click and drag the arrow displayed on the selected faces.

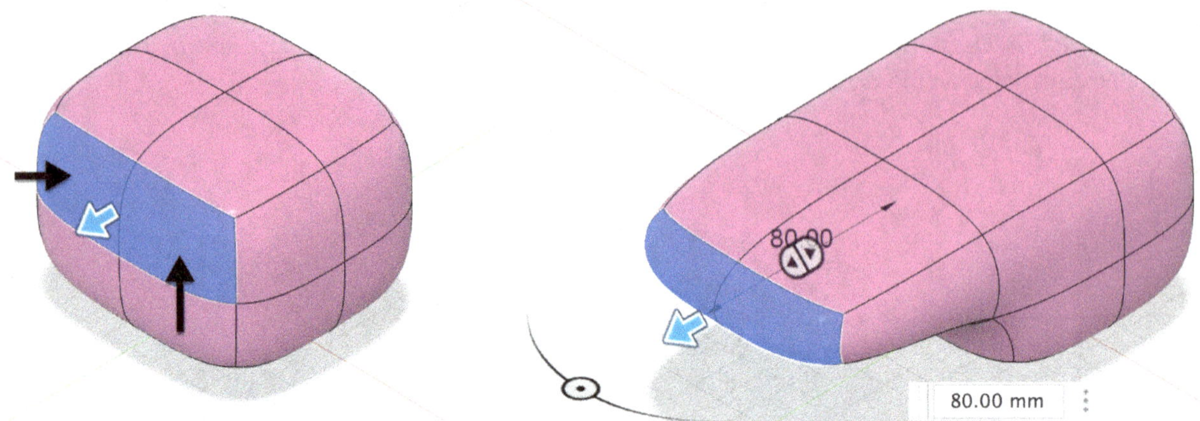

Notice that there is a smooth transition from the bottom of the extrusion. On the **Extrude** dialog, increase the value in the **Front Faces** box (or) click and drag the handle displayed on the extrusion; faces are added to the extrusion. Also, the smoothness is reduced as you increase the number of front faces.

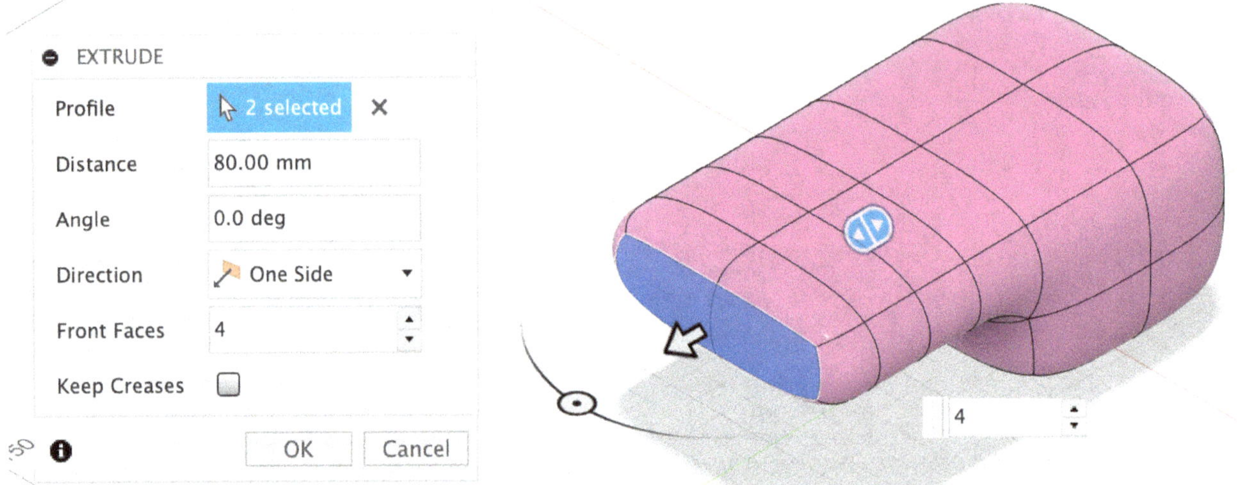

Extruding a Planar Face

Create a planar face using the **Plane** command. Next, activate the **Extrude** command and select all the faces of the planar face. Click and drag the arrow to add thickness to the face. Next, click **OK**.

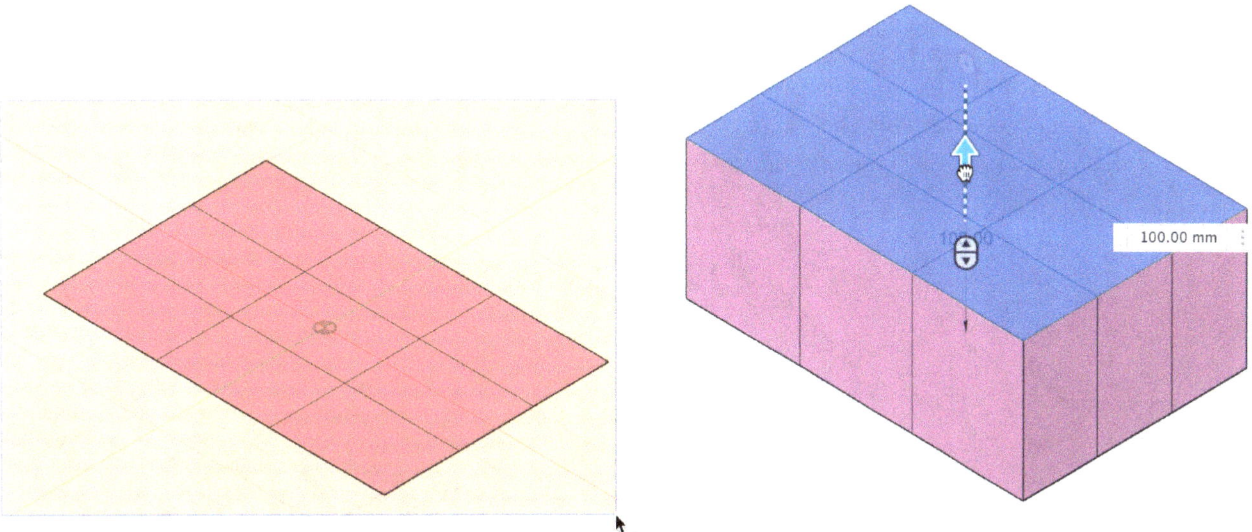

Activate the **Extrude** command and click on the right-corner face of the top face. Next, click and drag the arrow displayed on the selected face. Next, check the **Keep Creases** option and notice that the edges adjacent to the extruded face a straight. Uncheck the **Keep Creases** option and notice that the adjacent edges are distorted.

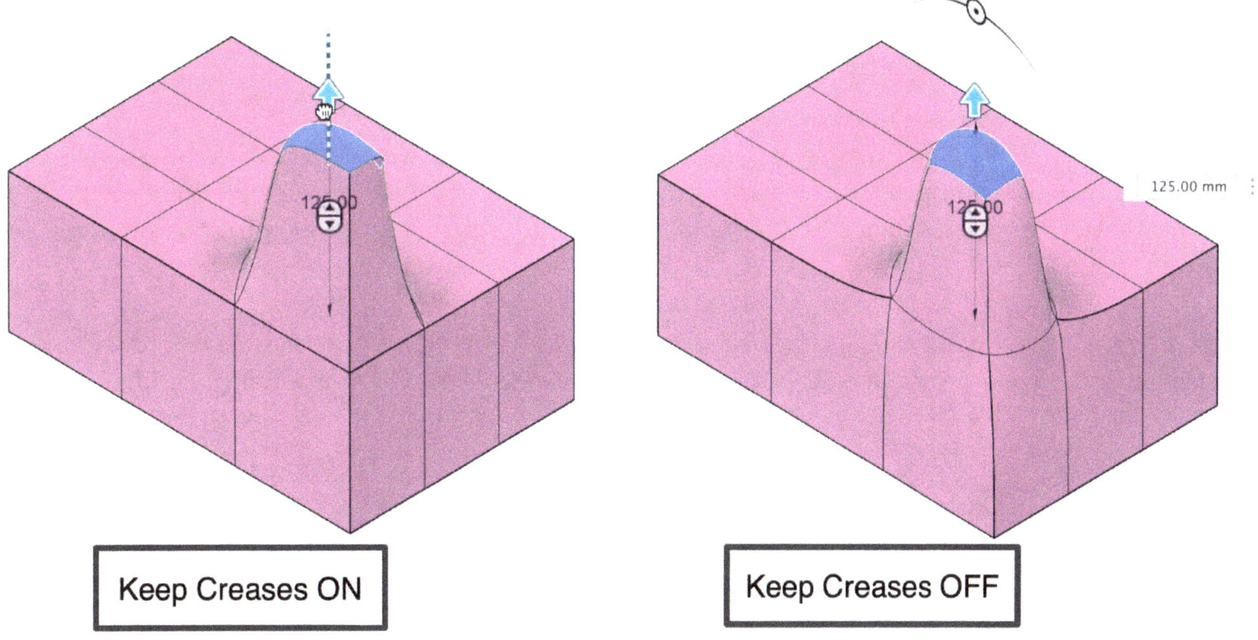

The Revolve command

The **Revolve** command revolves a sketch curve or edges of a T-spline surface. This command is practically illustrated in the following example. First, create a sketch and the axis of revolution. Activate the Revolve command (on the toolbar, click **Form > Create > Revolve**). Select the profile from the graphics window. On the **Revolve** dialog, click the **Axis** button and then select the axis line from the graphics window.

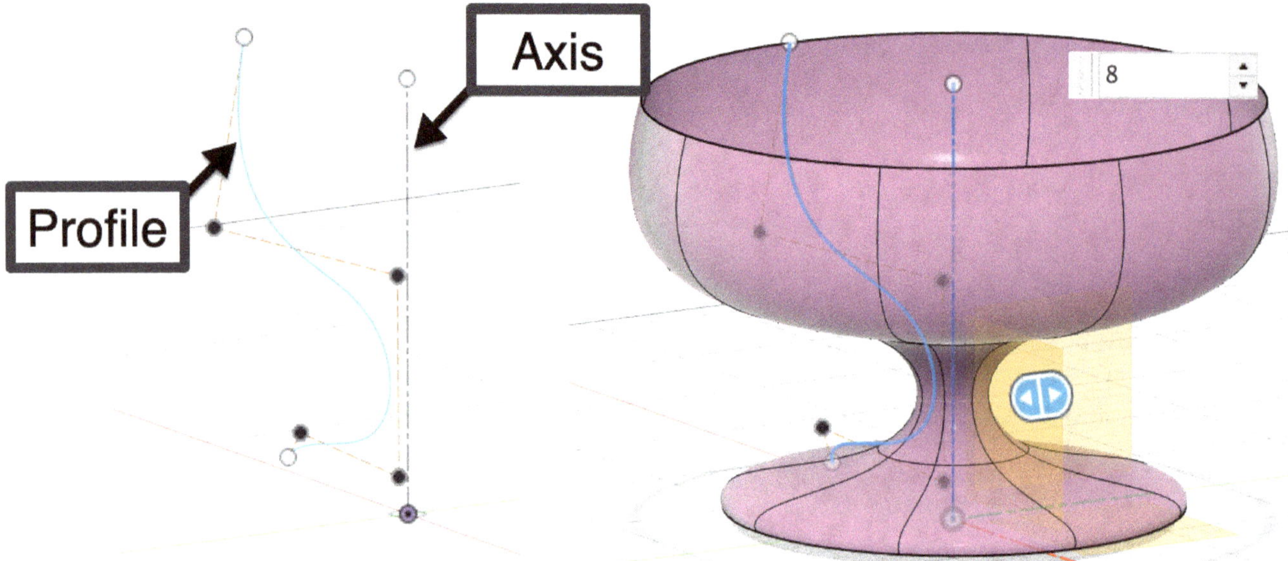

Select an option from the **Type** drop-down (Full or Angle). The **Full** option creates full 360 degree revolution. If you select the **Angle** option, you need to specify the angle of revolution. Next, type in a value in the **Faces** box. Note that the number of faces should be three or more. Click **OK** to create the revolved T-spline surface.

Edit Form

After creating the freeform primitive shapes, you need to manipulate them by transforming the edges. For example, create a quadball, as shown below. Elements of the T-spline surface are also shown in the figure.

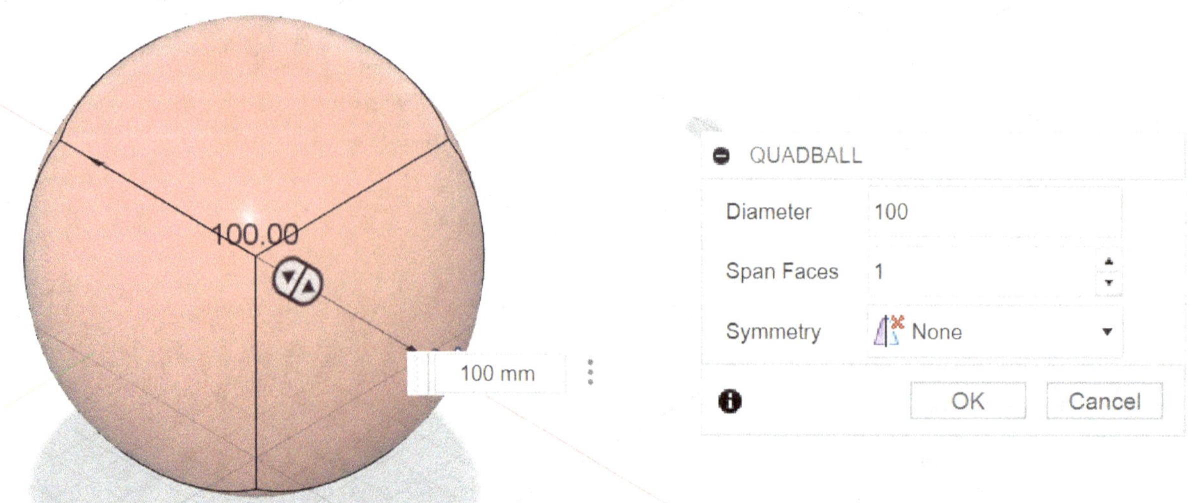

On the toolbar, click **Form > Modify > Edit Form** and select the right face of the quadball, as shown. On the **Edit Form** dialog, select **Transform Mode > Multi**; the manipulator is displayed on the selected face. Click and drag the arrow pointing in the direction perpendicular to the selected face. Release the pointer to move the selected face.

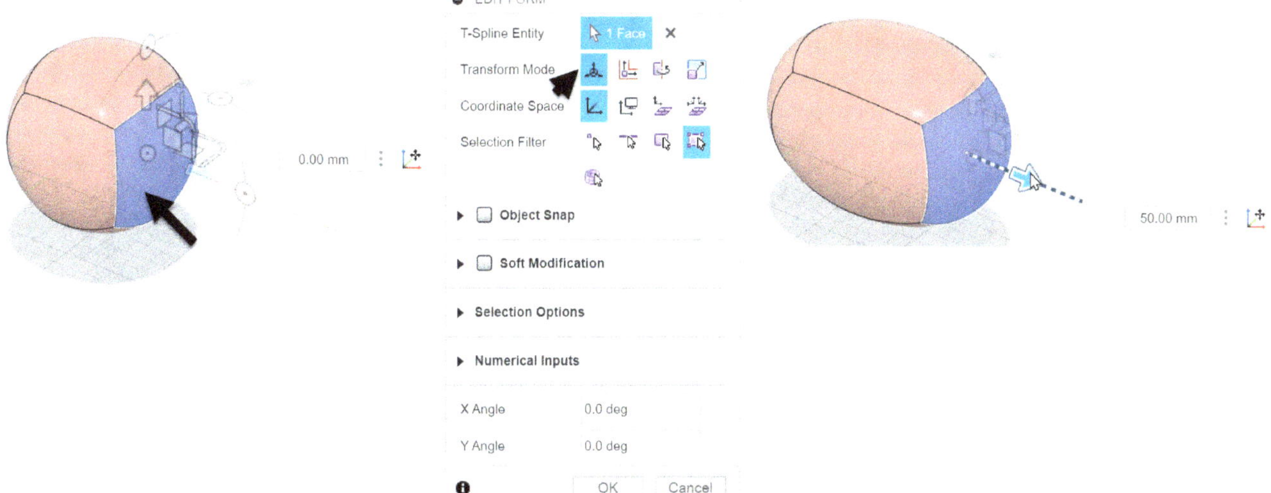

Press and hold the ALT key and drag the arrow displayed perpendicular to the selected face. Left-click to release the arrow; the selected face is extruded.

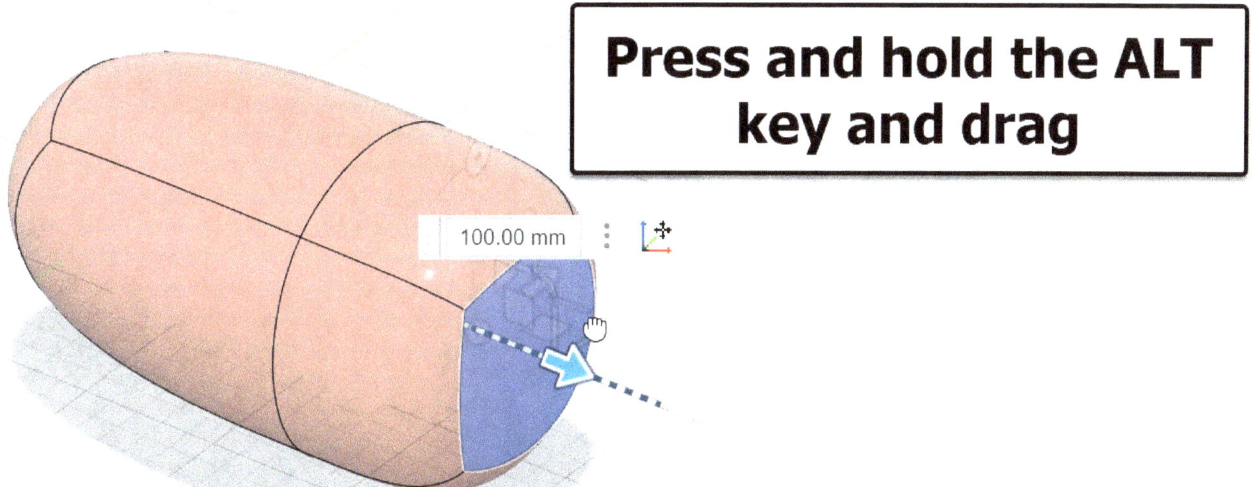

Click on the corner fillet of the plane of the manipulator. Next, press and hold the left mouse button and drag the corner fillet of the plane (Uniform scaling handle). Left-click and notice that the selected face is scaled uniformly.

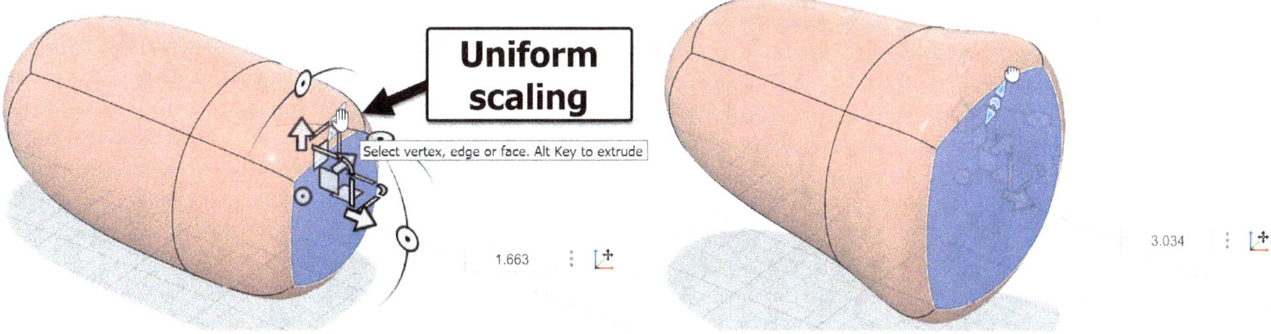

Click and drag the top edge of the plane of the manipulator; the selected face is scaled vertically.

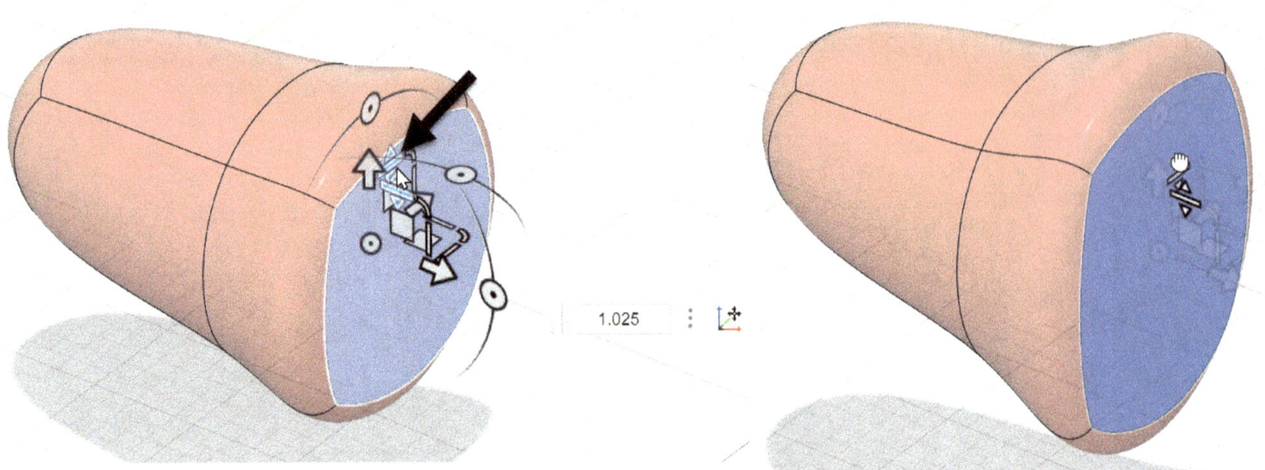

Click and drag the right edge of the plane of the manipulator; the selected face of the T-spline body is scaled horizontally.

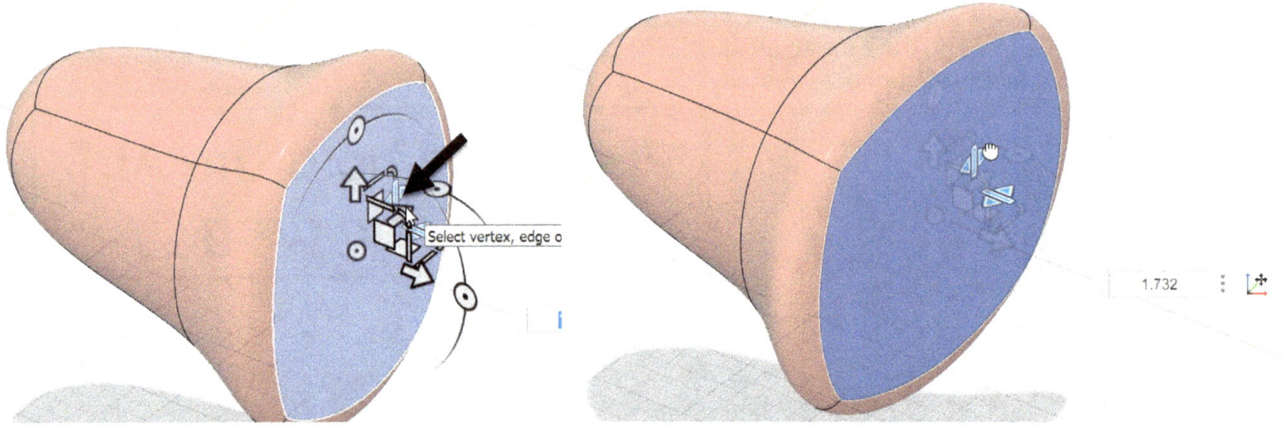

Create a box with the parameters, as shown.

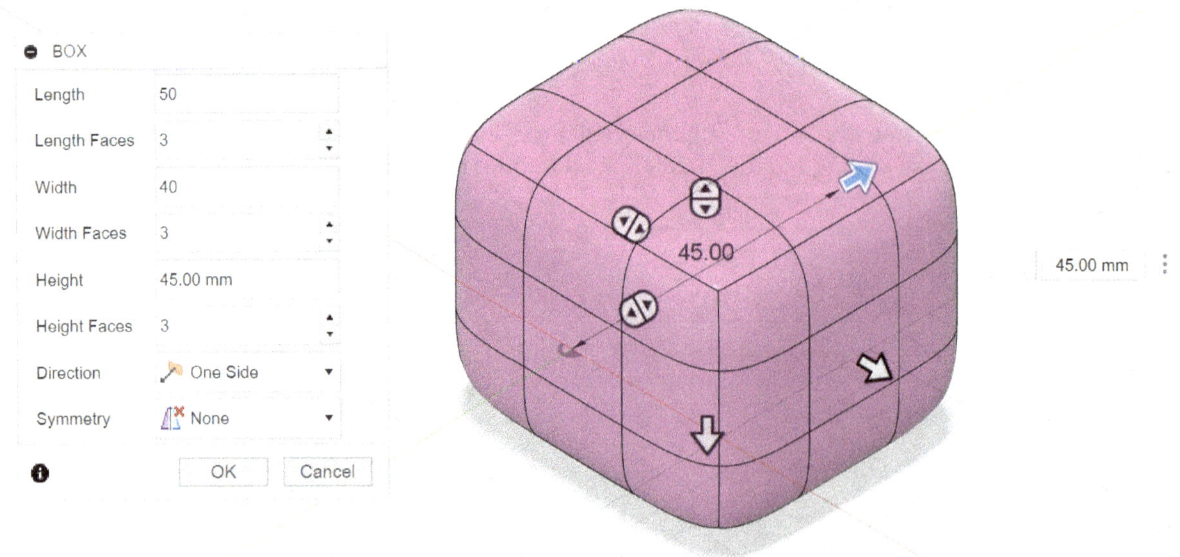

On the toolbar, click **Form > Modify > Edit Form** and click on the top-center face of the box, as shown. On the **Edit Form** dialog, expand the **Selection Options** section and click **Grow/Sink > Grow Selection** ; the surrounding faces of the selected face are selected. Again, click the Grow Selection icon; the faces surrounding the active selection are selected.

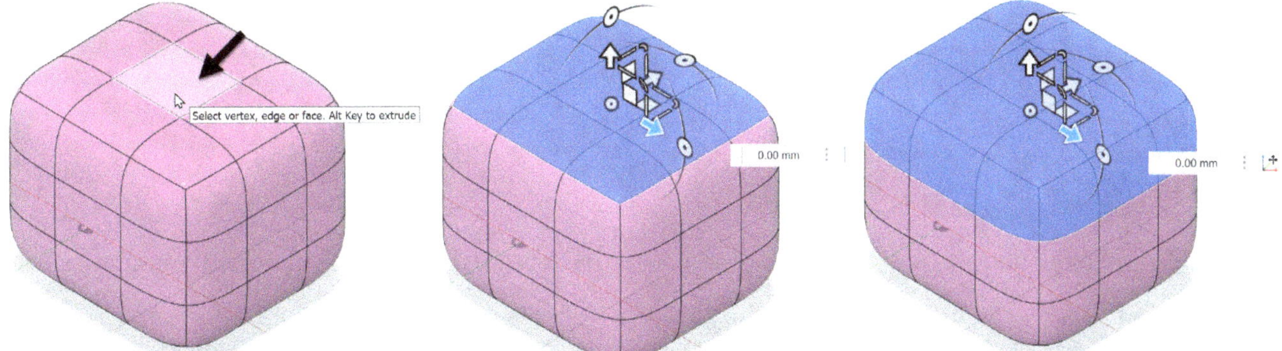

On the **Edit Form** dialog, click **Transform Mode > Rotation**; the Rotation manipulator is displayed on the selected faces. Click and drag the arrow handle pointing upward. Next, type-in a value in the **Angle** box.

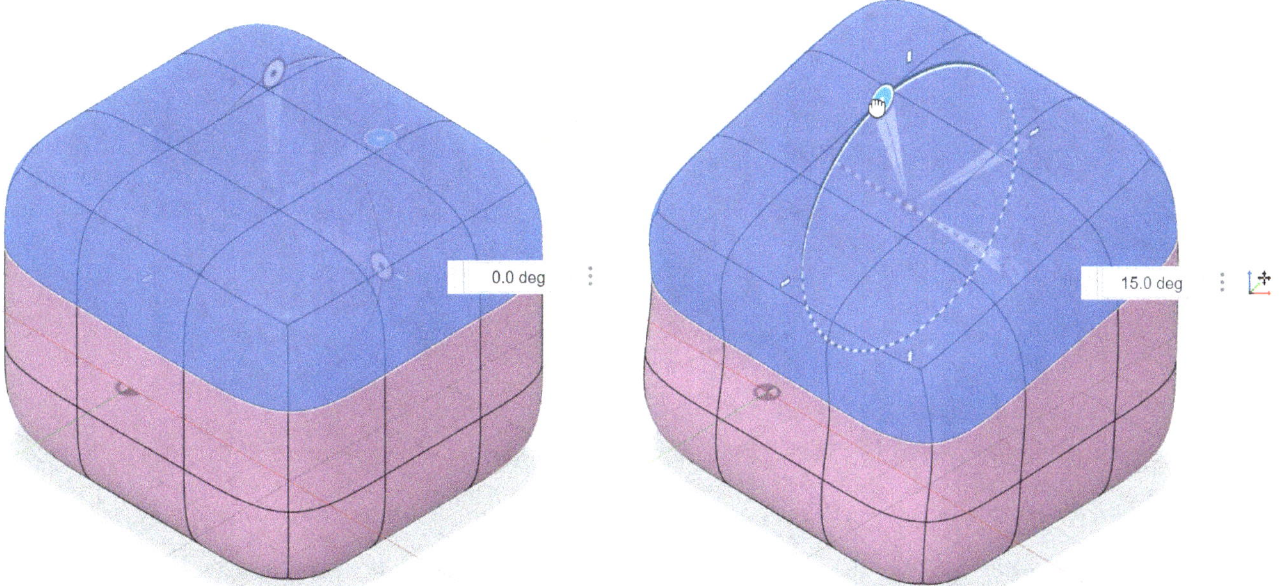

Click in the graphics window to deselect the selected faces. Select the edge, as shown. Next, expand the **Selection Options** section on the **Edit Form** dialog. Click **Loop Grow/Sink > Loop Selection** . The edge loop is selected.

On the **Edit Form** dialog, click **Transform mode > Scale** . Click and drag the fillet corner of the bottom plane; the edge loop is scaled.

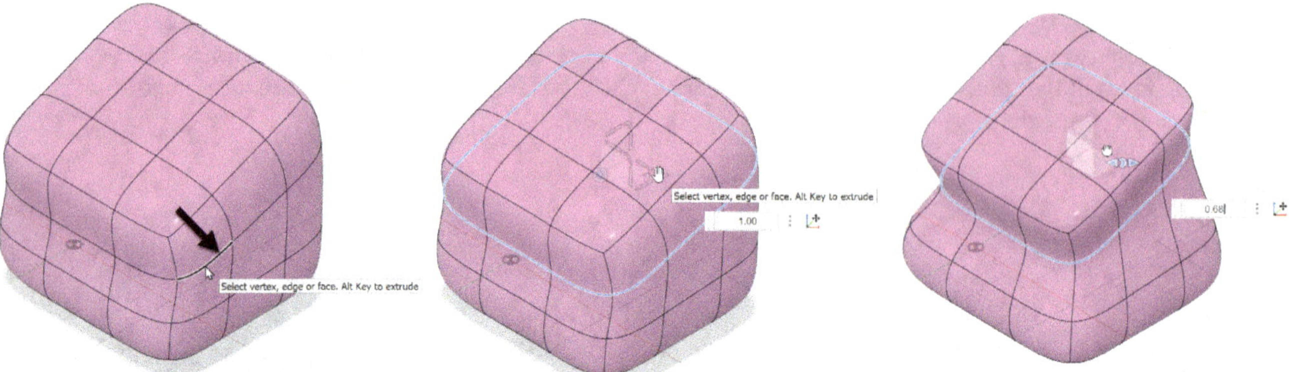

Click in the graphics window to deselect the edge loop. Next, select the edge of the T-spline body, as shown. On

the **Edit Form** dialog, expand the **Selection Options** section and click **Ring Grow/Shrink > Ring Selection** ; the edges parallel to the selected edge are selected. Click on the fillet edge of the horizontal plane of the scale manipulator. Press and hold the left mouse button and drag the pointer; the selected edges are scaled.

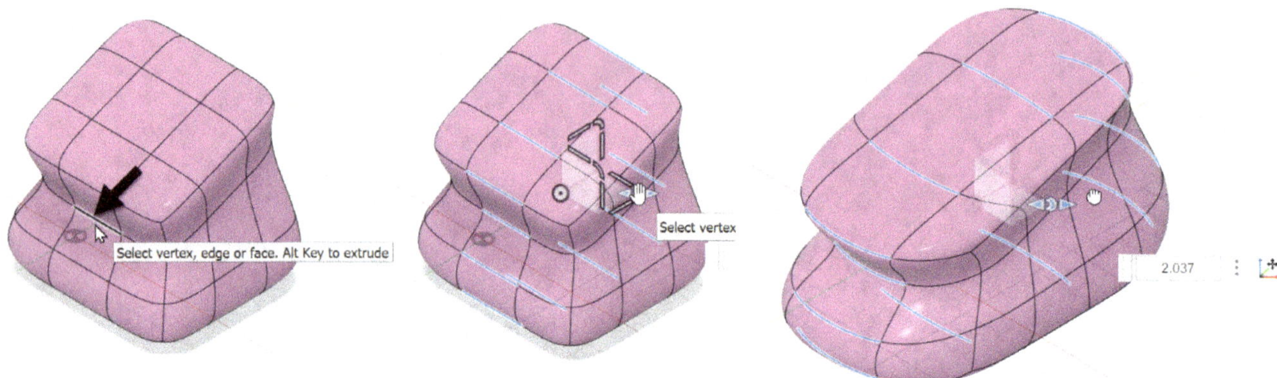

Click in the graphics window to deselect the selected edges. Next, click on the center face of the top inclined face, as shown. On the **Edit Form** dialog, select Transform Mode > Translation . On the **Edit Form** dialog, select **Coordinate Space > World Space** ; the manipulator orients to the world coordinate system. Select **Coordinate Space > View Space** ; the manipulator is oriented to the active view. Select **Coordinate Space > Selection Space** ; the manipulator is oriented to the selected face.

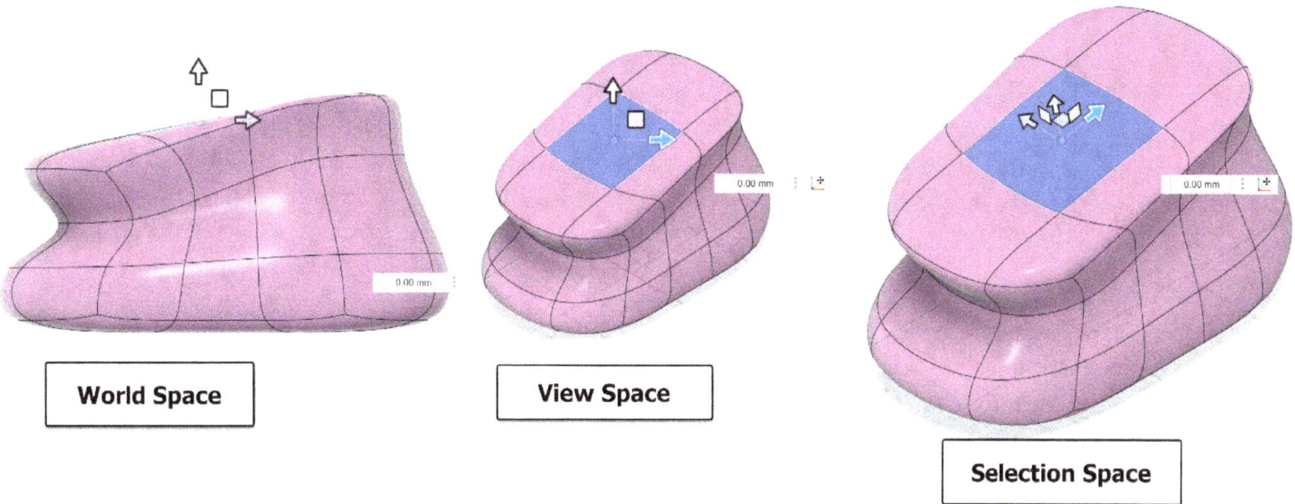

Click and drag the arrow pointing upwards.

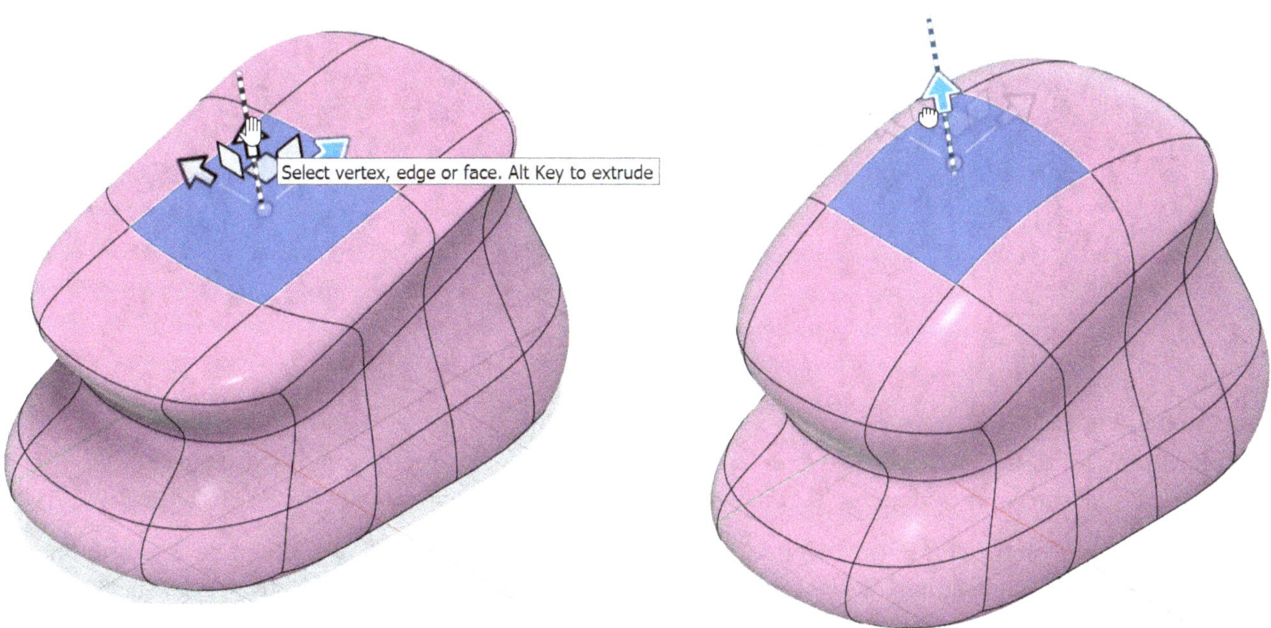

Activate the **Edit Form** command and select a face, as shown. Next, expand the **Selection Options** section on the

Edit Form dialog and select the **Feature Selection** icon; the entire feature associated with the selected face is selected. Next, click and drag the horizontal arrow of the manipulator; the selected feature is moved.

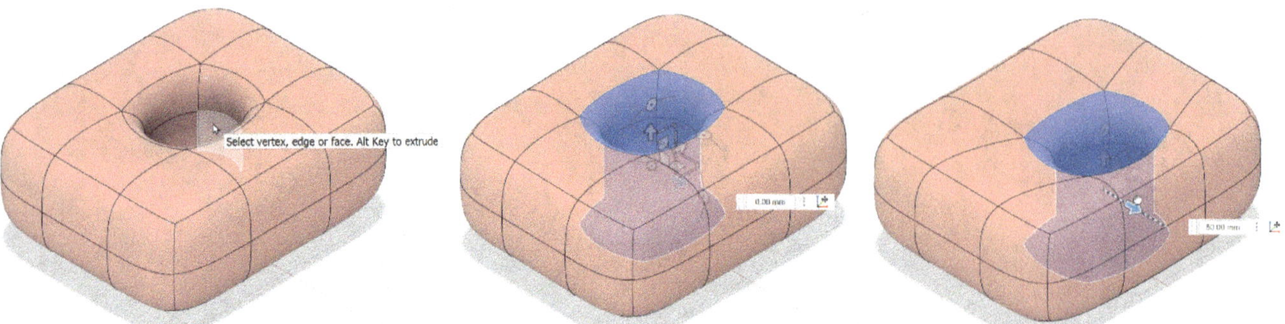

Click the **Invert Selection** icon on the **Selection Options** section; the selection is inverted. Click and drag the scale handle of the manipulator to scale the selection.

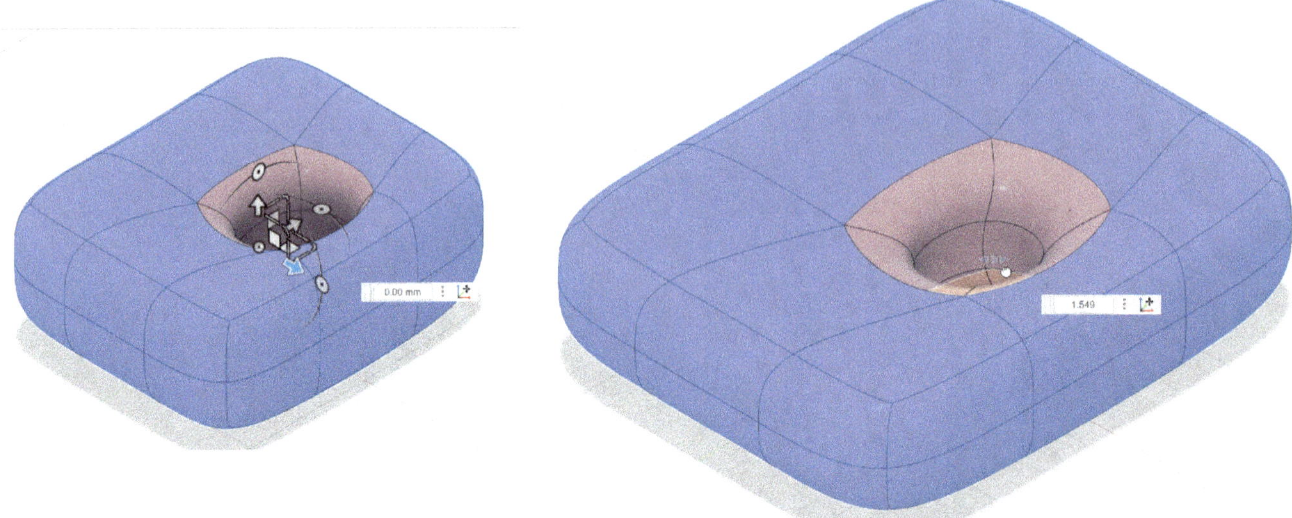

Soft Modification

The **Soft Modification** options allow you to deform a T-spline body by manipulating a face, edge or edge. Activate the Edit Form command and select the vertex of the T-spline surface, as shown. Next, check the **Soft Modification** option on the **Edit Form** dialog. Click **Extent > Distance** ; the edges and vertices surrounding the selected vertex are highlighted in red. You can determine the range of highlighted edges by specifying a value in the **Distance** box.

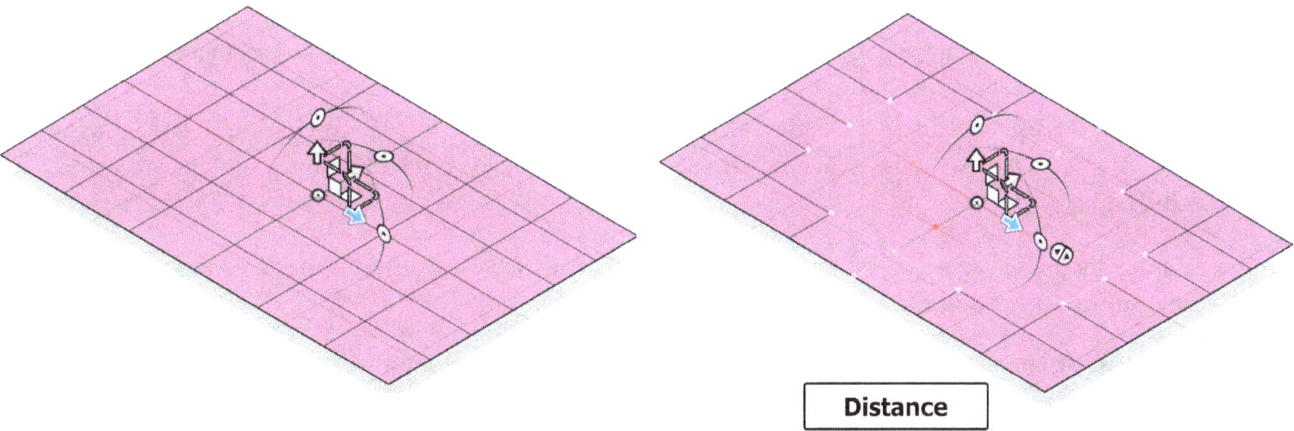

Click **Extent > Face Count** and specify the number of faces to be affected in the **Face Count** box. Click **Extent > Rectangular Face Count** and specify the **Length Face Count** and **Width Face Count** values.

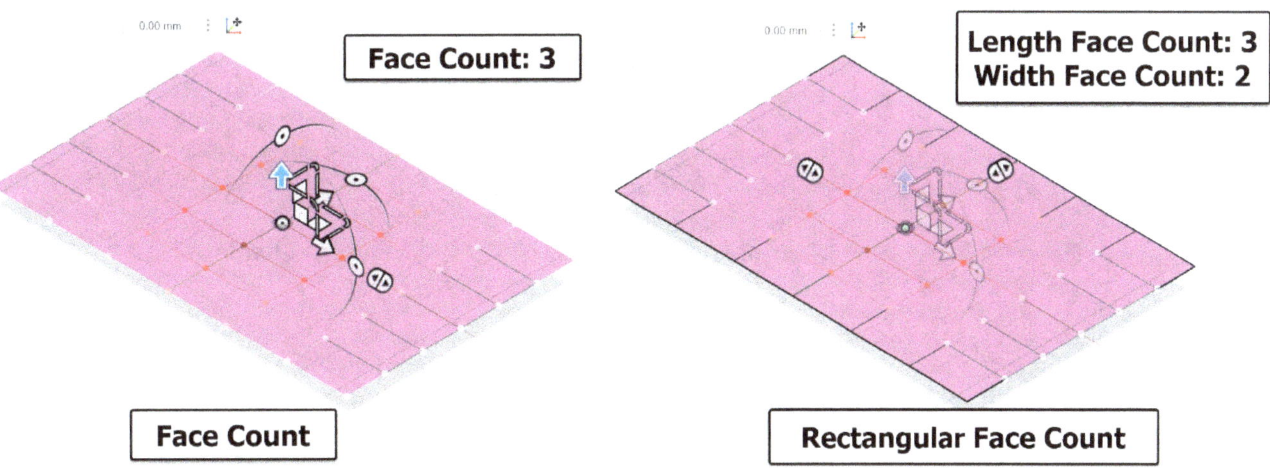

Click and drag the manipulator arrow pointing upward; the shape of the T-spline surface deformed. Notice that the deformation is more at the selected point. The deformation reduces gradually at the outer edges. This is because the **Transition** is set to **Smooth**. Select **Transition > Linear**; this will slightly increase the deformation at the outer edges. Select **Transition > Bulge**; This will cause the deformation at the outer edge of the affected area to be greater than with the **Linear** option, resulting in a bulge.

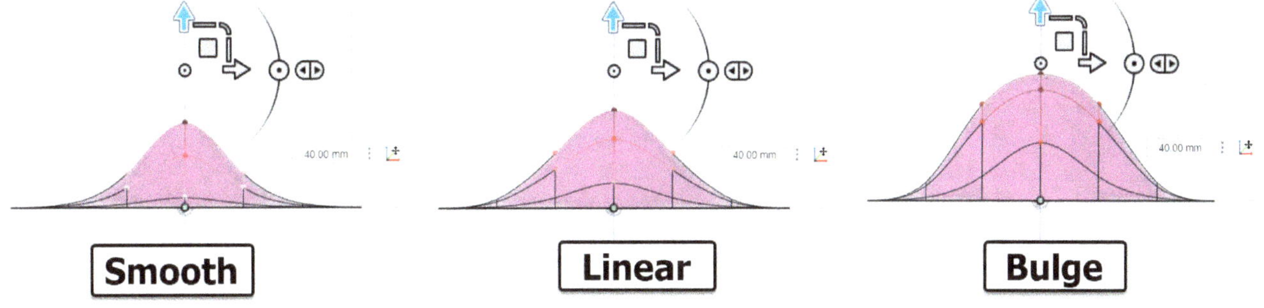

Specify the **Weight** value by entering a value in the **Weight** box of dragging the slider. Notice that the number edge highlighted in red increases as you increase the **Weight** value.

Display Mode

The **Display Mode** command helps you to change the display of the edges of the T-spline. Activate this command

(on the toolbar, click **Form > Utilities > Display Mode**   ) and select the display mode from the **Display Mode** dialog. There are three Display Modes available: **Box Display Control +1**, **Control Frame Display Control +2**, and **Smooth Display Control +3**.

The **Box Display** mode displays the T-spline in low resolution with sharp edges. This mode allows you to edit large T-spline surfaces very quickly.

The **Control Frame Display** mode displays a smooth T-spline surface along with the control frame. You can edit the T-spline using the control frame edges and vertices.

The **Smooth Display** mode displays the T-spline with smooth edges.

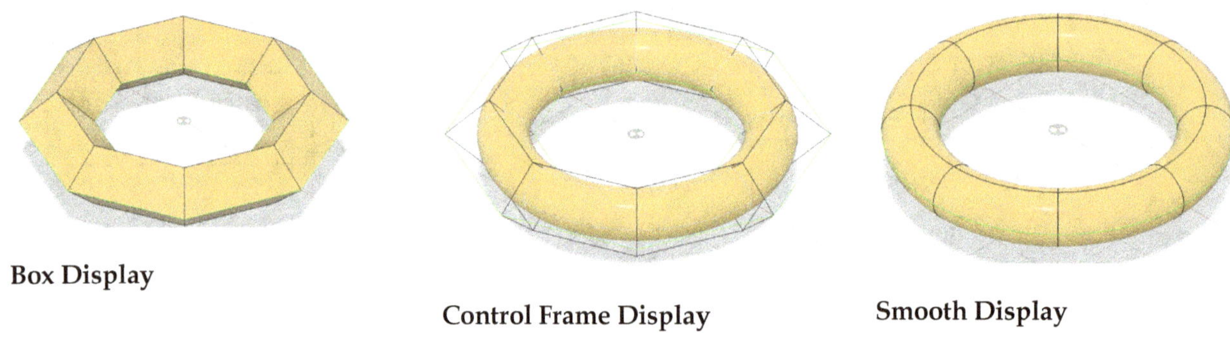

Box Display

Control Frame Display

Smooth Display

Edit By Curve

The **Edit By Curve** command helps you to edit the edges of a T-spline. For example, create a plane T-spline surface, as shown. Next, activate this command (on the toolbar, click **Form > Modify > Edit By Curve**   ) and select the edges of the plane, as shown. Next, click the **Curve Control Points** selection button; the curve and control points are displayed on the selected edge. On the **Edit By Curve** dialog, type 3 in the Degree box (or) use the Degree slider to adjust the degree of the control points. It is easy to edit the selected edges if the number of degree is greater than the number of selected edges.

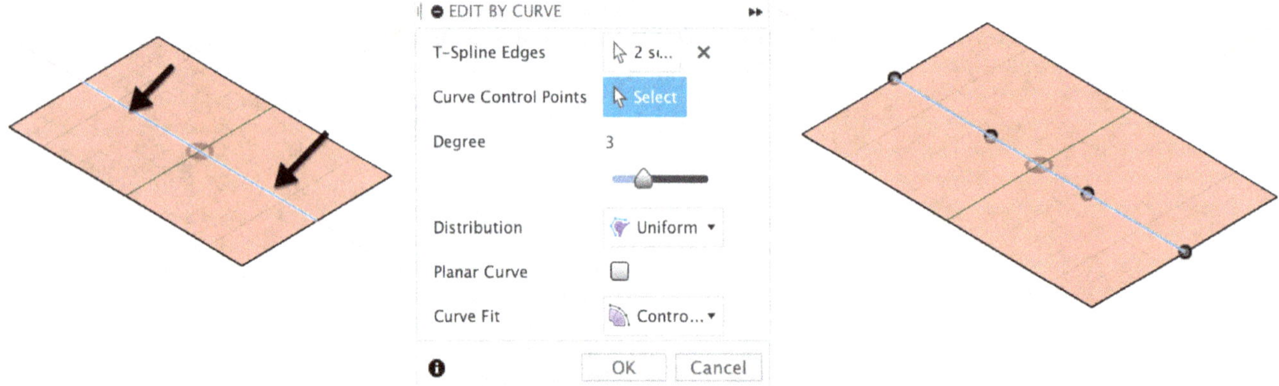

Select the control point displayed on the selected edge, as shown. Next, click and drag the arrow pointing in the upward direction; the control point is moved upward. Also, the curve is modified.

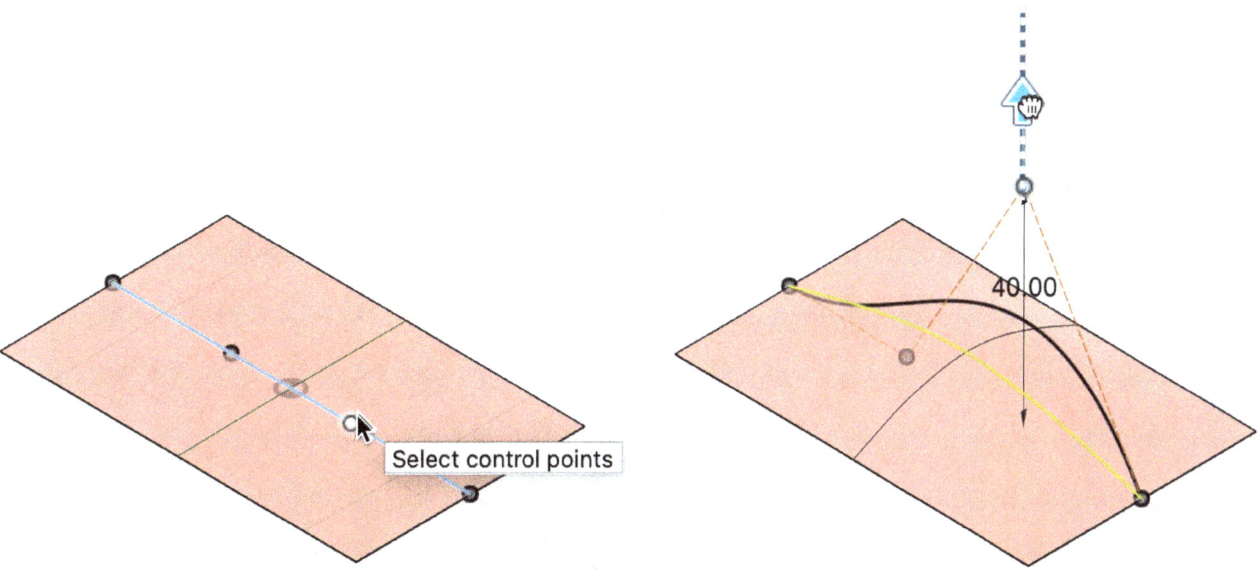

You can also click and drag the plane of the manipulator, as shown.

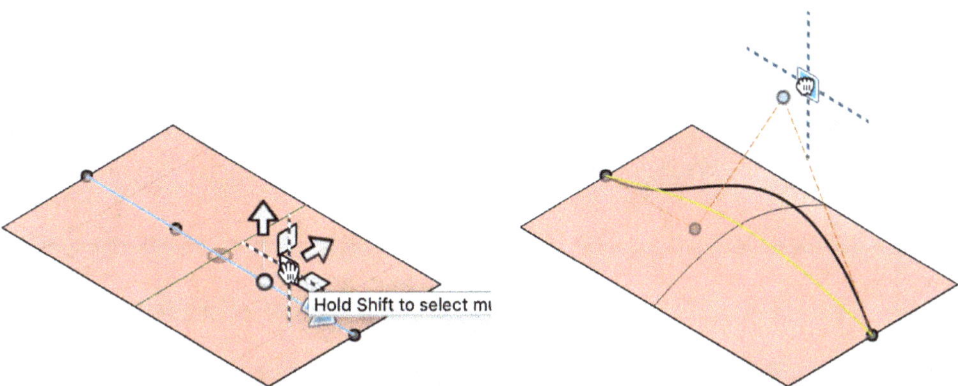

Select an option from the **Distribution** drop-down. The **Uniform** option distributes the control points uniformly along the curve. The **Edge Length** option distributes the control point equally along the length of the selected edge.

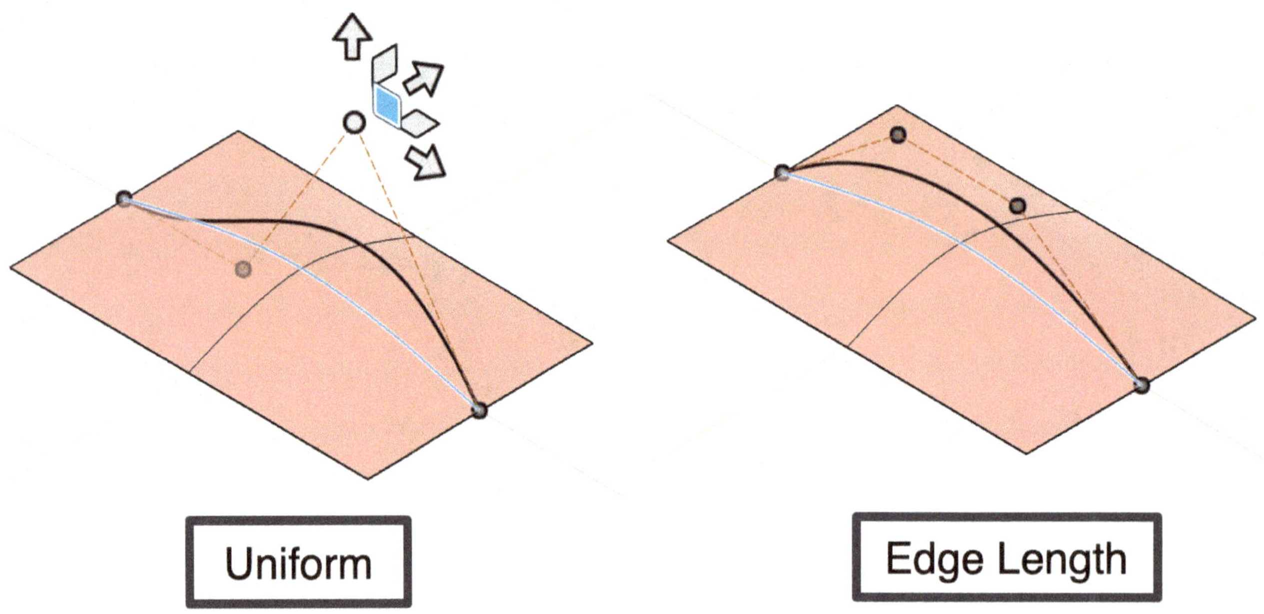

Select **Curve Fit > Surface points**; the curve is fitted on the surface.

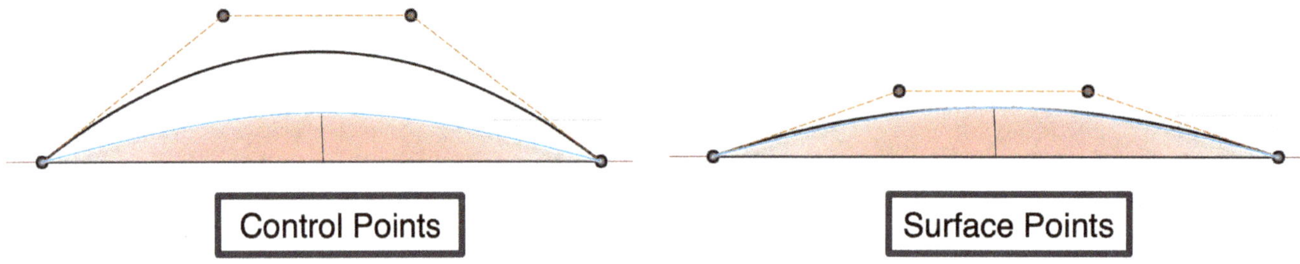

Expand the **Numerical Inputs** section on the **Edit By Curve** dialog. Next, select a control point, click and drag the plane of the manipulator; the values in the Numerical Inputs section change. You can also type-in values in the **X Distance**, **Y Distance**, and **Z Distance** boxes to specify the new location of the control point.

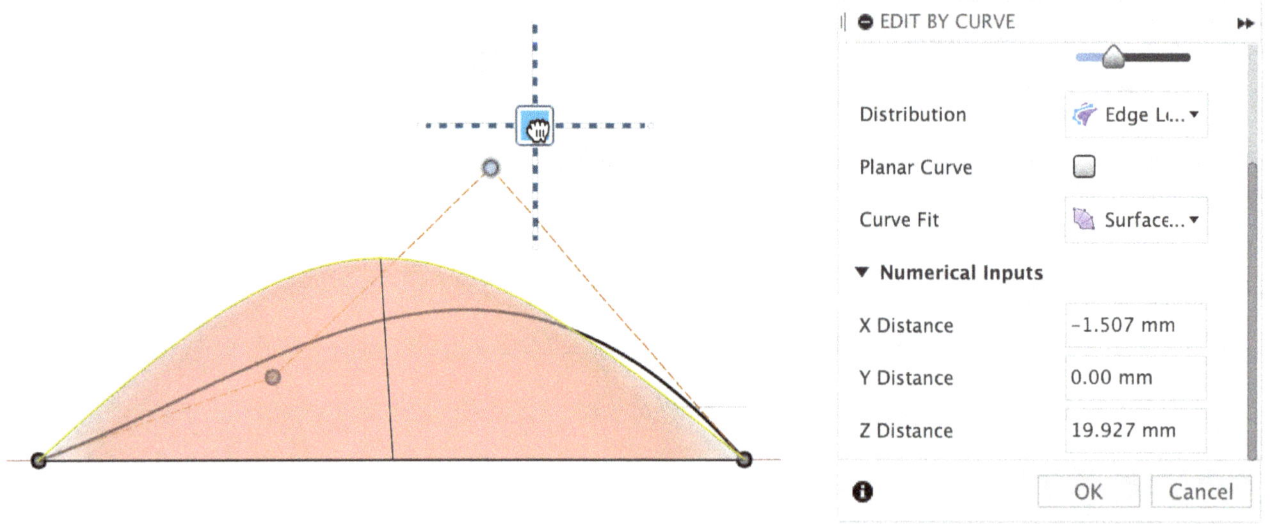

Flatten

The **Flatten** command completely flattens the selected faces of a T-spline body. Select the faces to flatten and click

Form > Modify > Flatten   on the toolbar. On the **Flatten** dialog, select the **Fit** option from the **Direction** drop-down. You can also select the **Select Plane** or **Select Parallel Plane** option to specify the orientation of the flatten surface by selecting a reference plane.

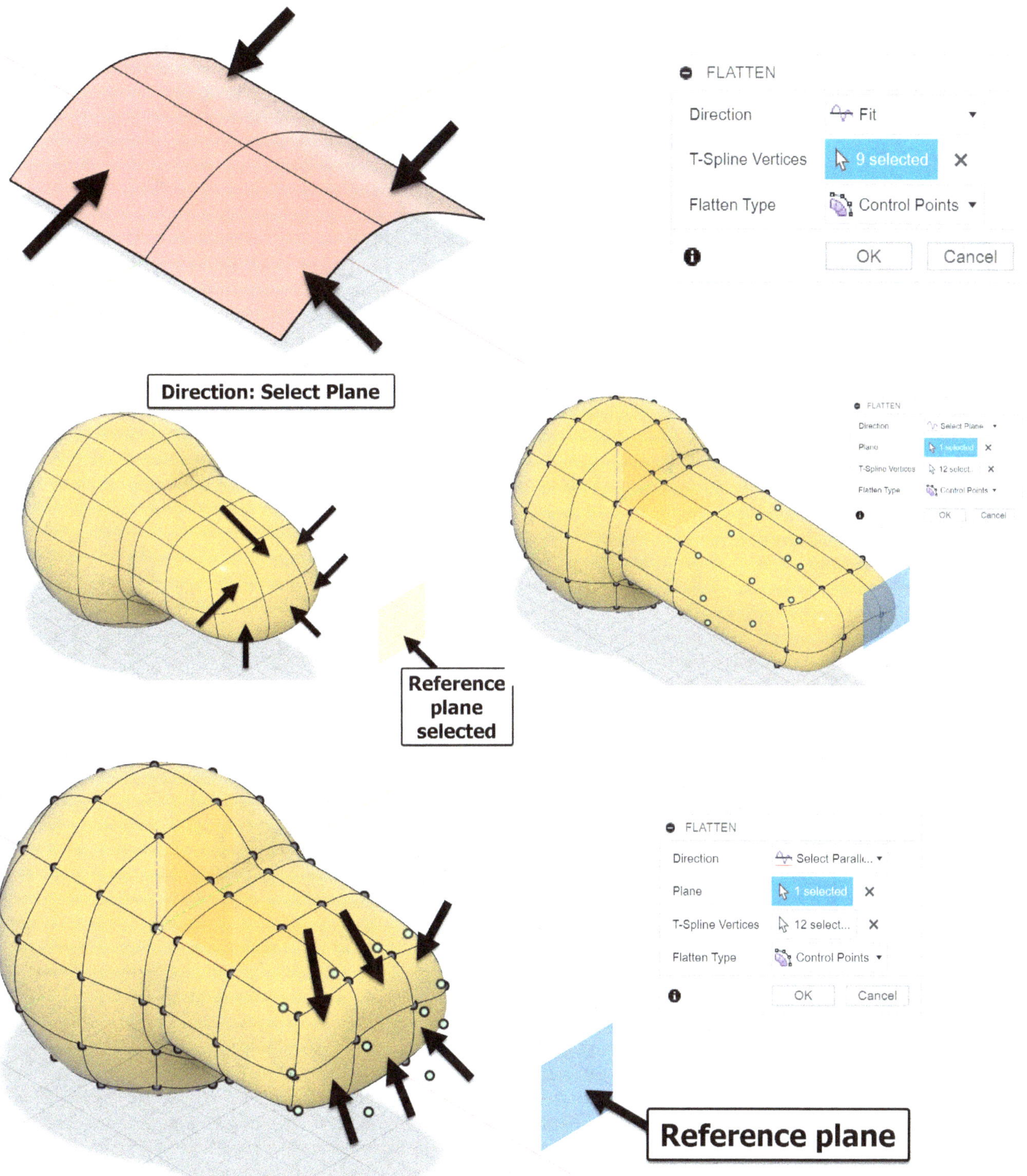

Select an option from the **Flatten Type** dialog. The **Control Points** option flattens the control vertices of the selected faces. The **Surface Points** option flattens the surface points. Click **OK** on the **Flatten** dialog.

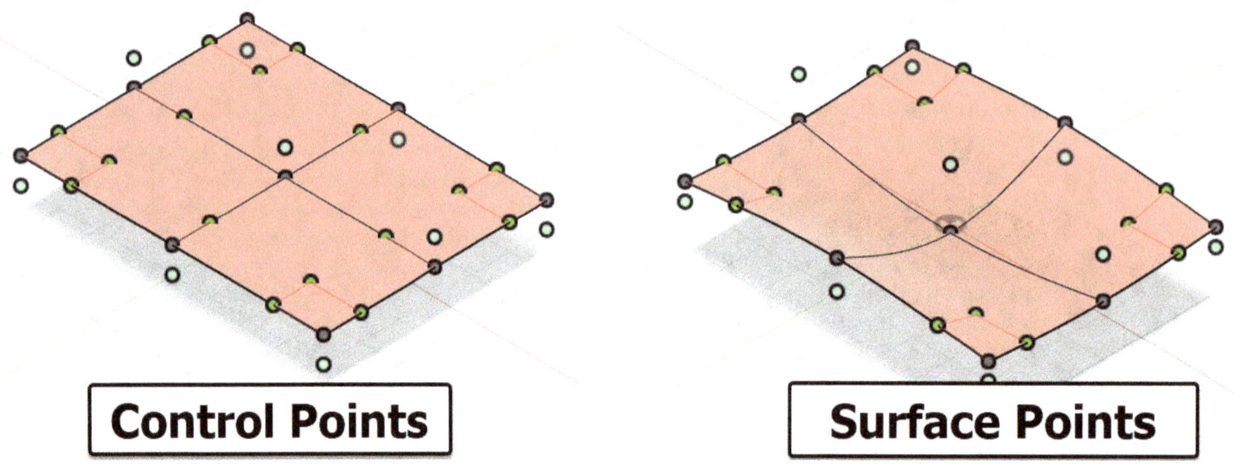

Straighten

The **Straighten** command straightens the selected edge of a T-spline body. Select an edge of a T-spline body

(double-click on the edge to select the connected edges) and click **Form > Modify > Straighten** on the toolbar. On the **Straighten** dialog, select the **Fit** option from the **Direction** drop-down. You can also select the **Select Line, Select Parallel line**, or **Select Two Points** option to specify the orientation of the straightened edge by selecting a line.

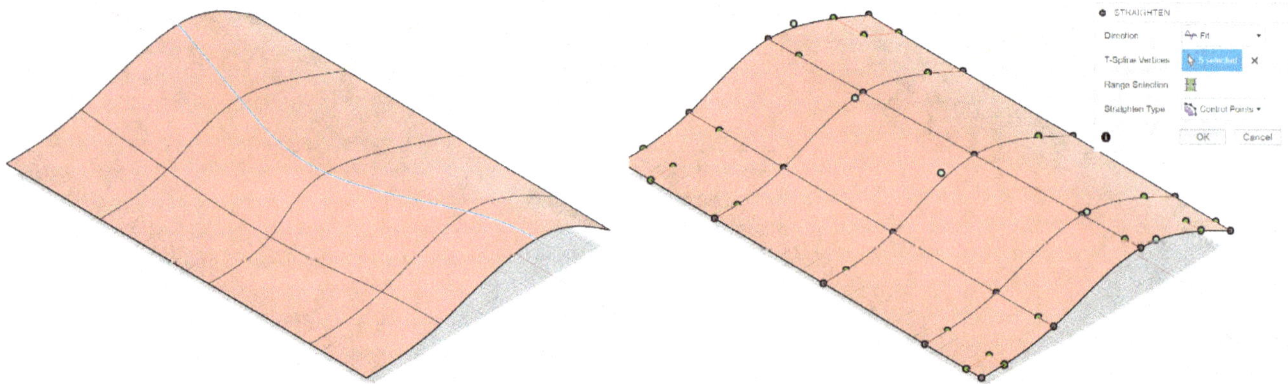

Mirror Internal

The **Mirror Internal** command helps you to make faces of a T-spline symmetrical about a plane. Activate this command (on the toolbar, click **Form > Symmetry > Mirror Internal**) and select the faces to be symmetrical. Next, click **OK**.

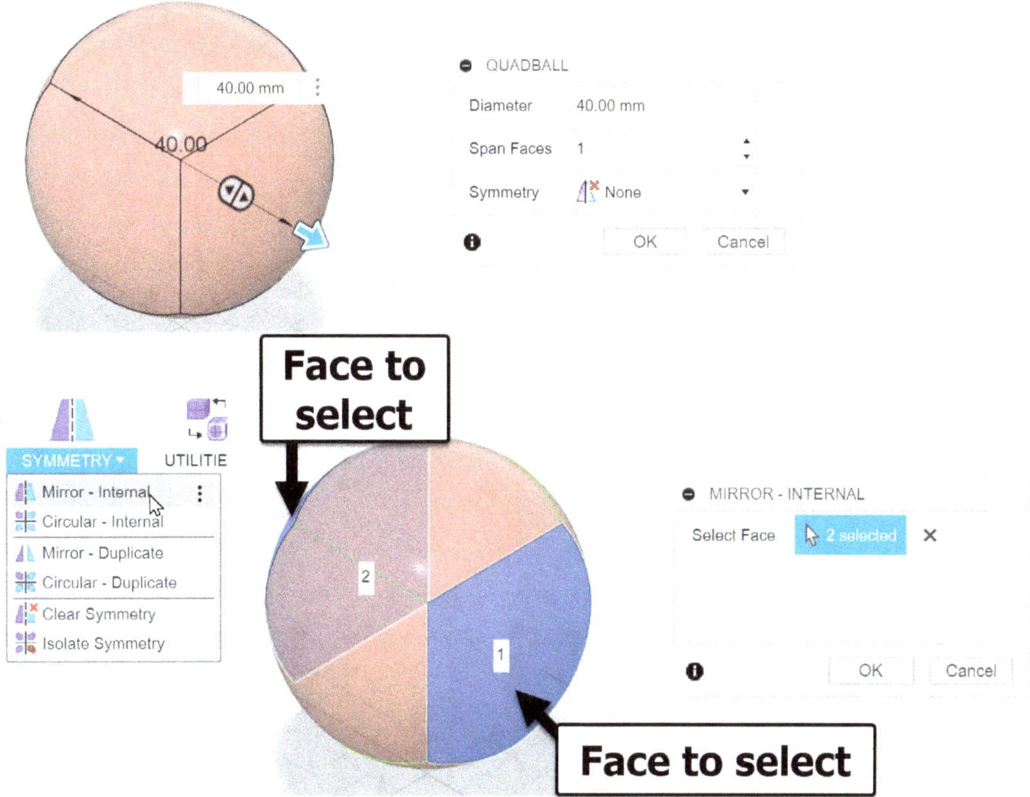

Now, activate the Edit Form command click on the side face of the quadball and notice an arrow. Press and hold the ALT key on your keyboard, cliick and drag the arrow toward the right; the selected face is extruded symmetrically on both sides. Click in the graphics window.

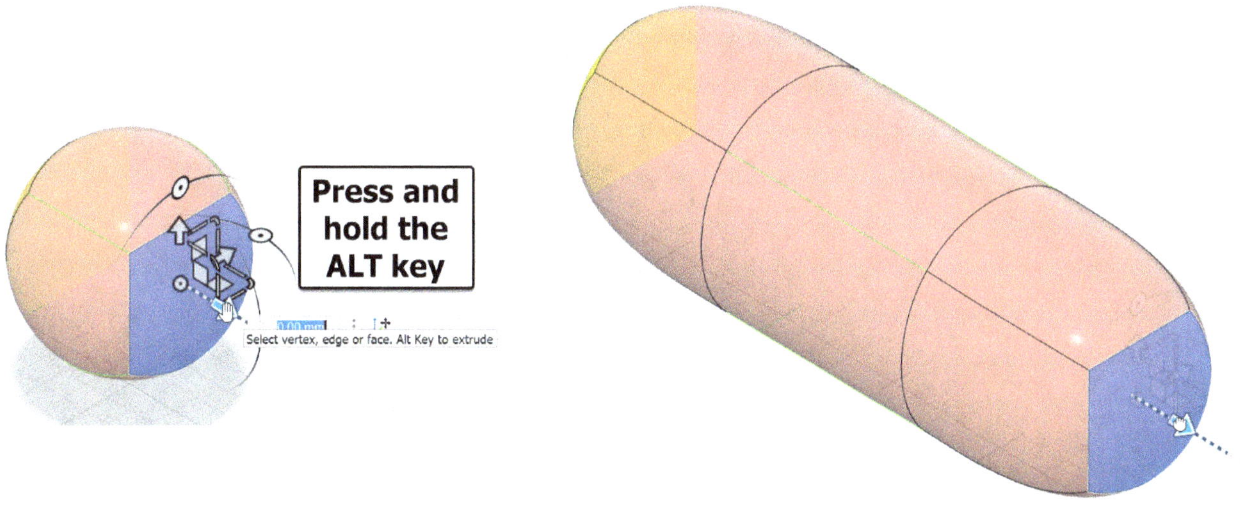

Select the right vertical edge of the cage and drag it in the forward direction.

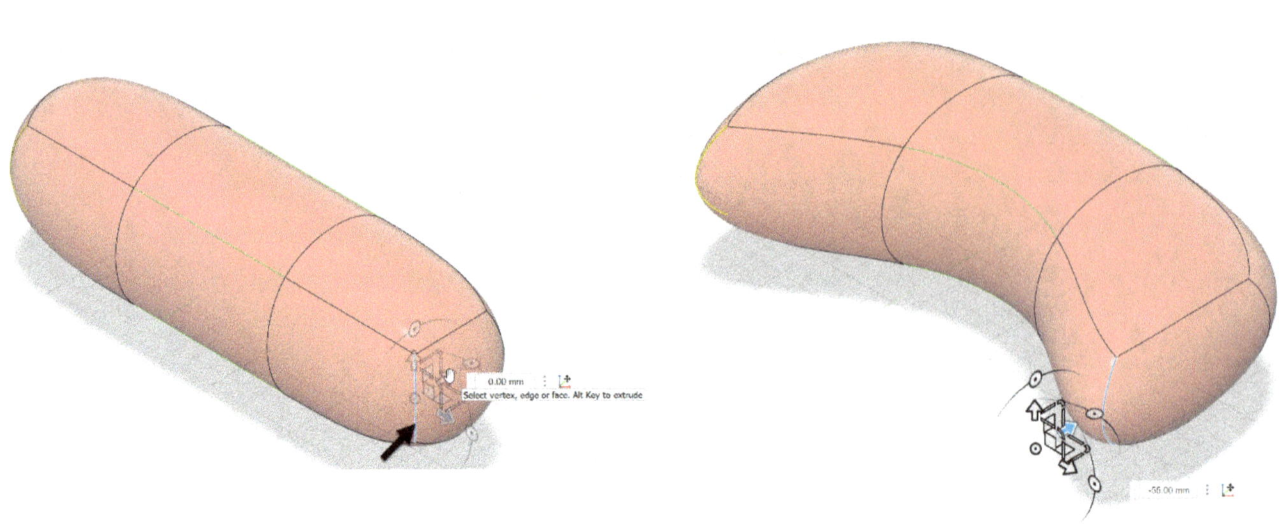

Clear Symmetry

You can use the **Clear Symmetry** command to stop manipulating the model symmetrically. Activate this command (on the toolbar, click **Form > Symmetry > Clear Symmetry**) and select the T-spline body. Click **OK** on the **Clear Symmetry** dialog. You can manipulate the model independently on both sides.

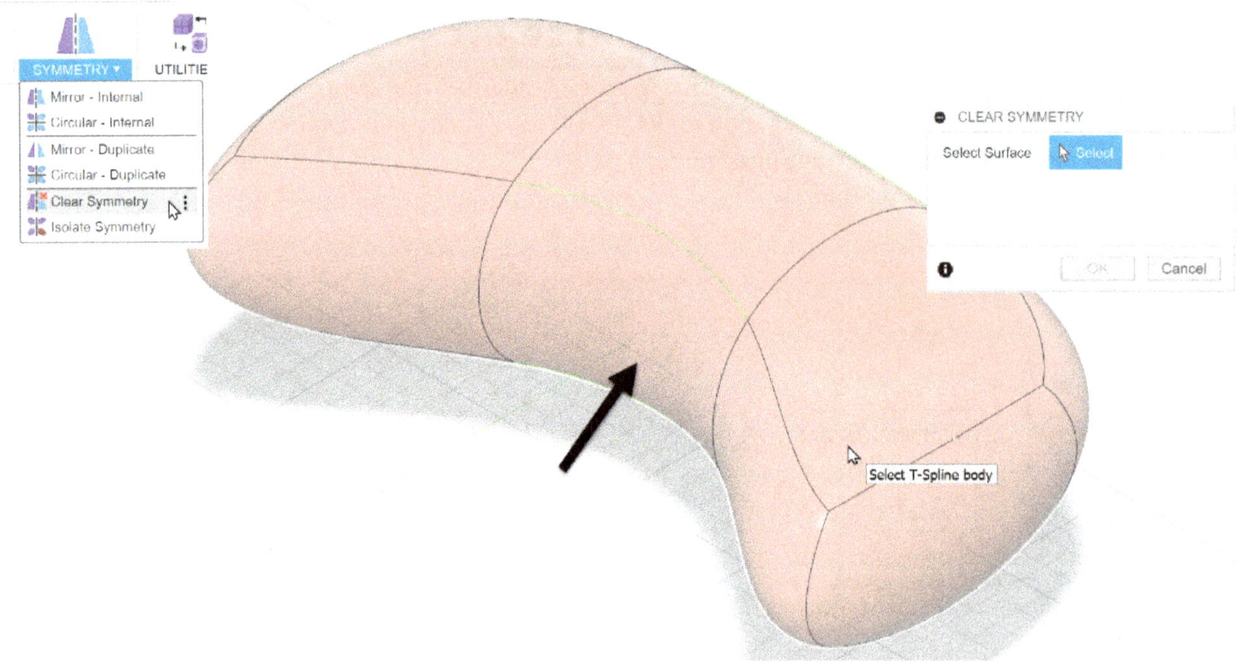

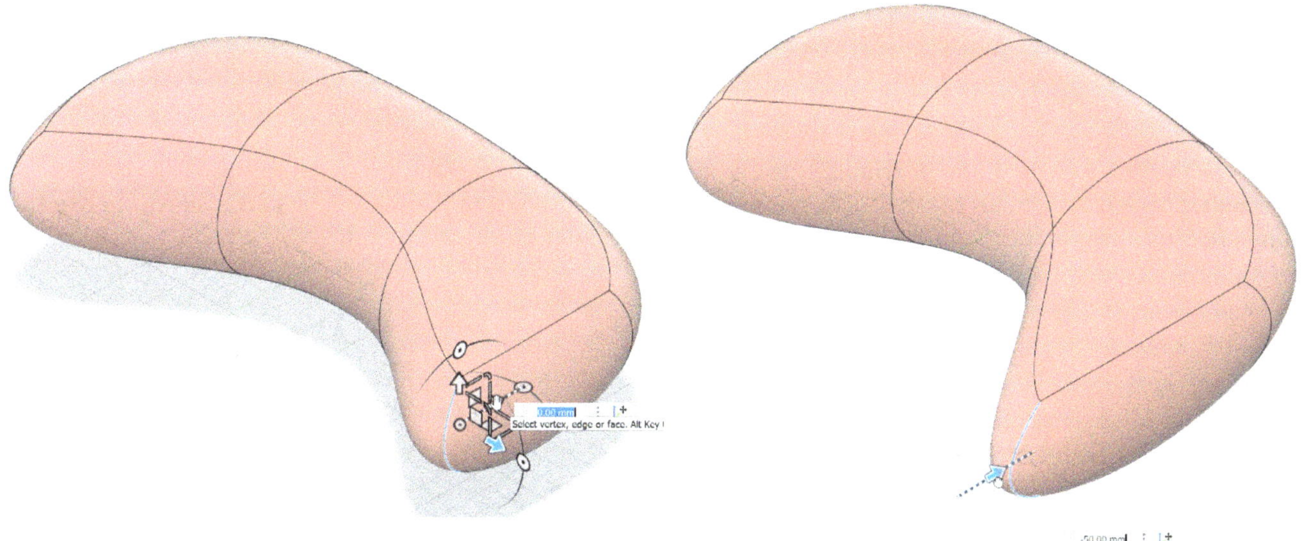

Circular Internal

The **Circular Internal** command helps you to apply circular symmetry between the faces of the T-spline body . Activate this command (on the toolbar, click **Form > Symmetry > Circular Internal**) and select a face from the T-spline body. Next, select an option (**2-sided symmetry**, **4-sided symmetry**, or **8-sided symmetry**) from the **Possible symmetries** drop-down. Click **OK** to create the circular symmetry.

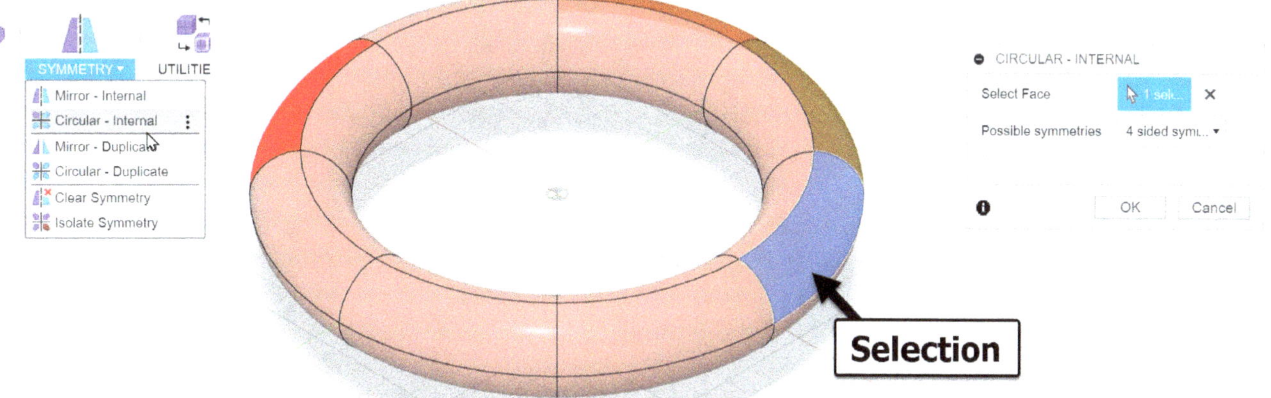

Activate the **Edit Form** command and select the face selected to create the circular internal symmetry. Next, click and drag the arrow displayed on the selected face; notice that the faces that are in circular symmetry with the selected face also move.

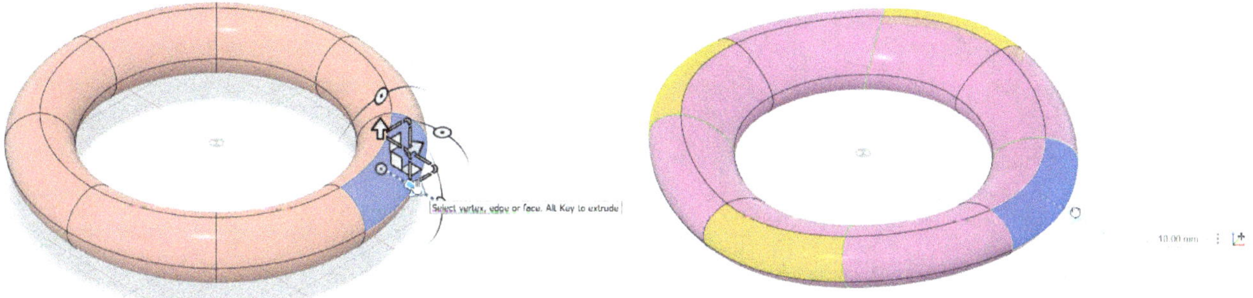

Circular Duplicate

The **Circular Duplicate** command helps you to create a circular pattern of the T-spline body. Activate this command (on the toolbar, click **Form > Symmetry > Circular Duplicate**) and select a T-spline body. Next, select the axis of the circular pattern. On the **Circular Duplicate** dialog, select an option (**Full, Partial,** or **Symmetric**) from the **Distribution** drop-down. The **Full** option distributes the instances of the circular pattern on full 360-degree angle. The **Partial** option distributes the instances of the circular pattern up to the specified angle. The **Symmetric** option distributes the instances symmetrically on both sides of the selected instance. Next, specify the number of instances in the **Quantity** box. Click **OK** on the **Circular Duplicate** dialog.

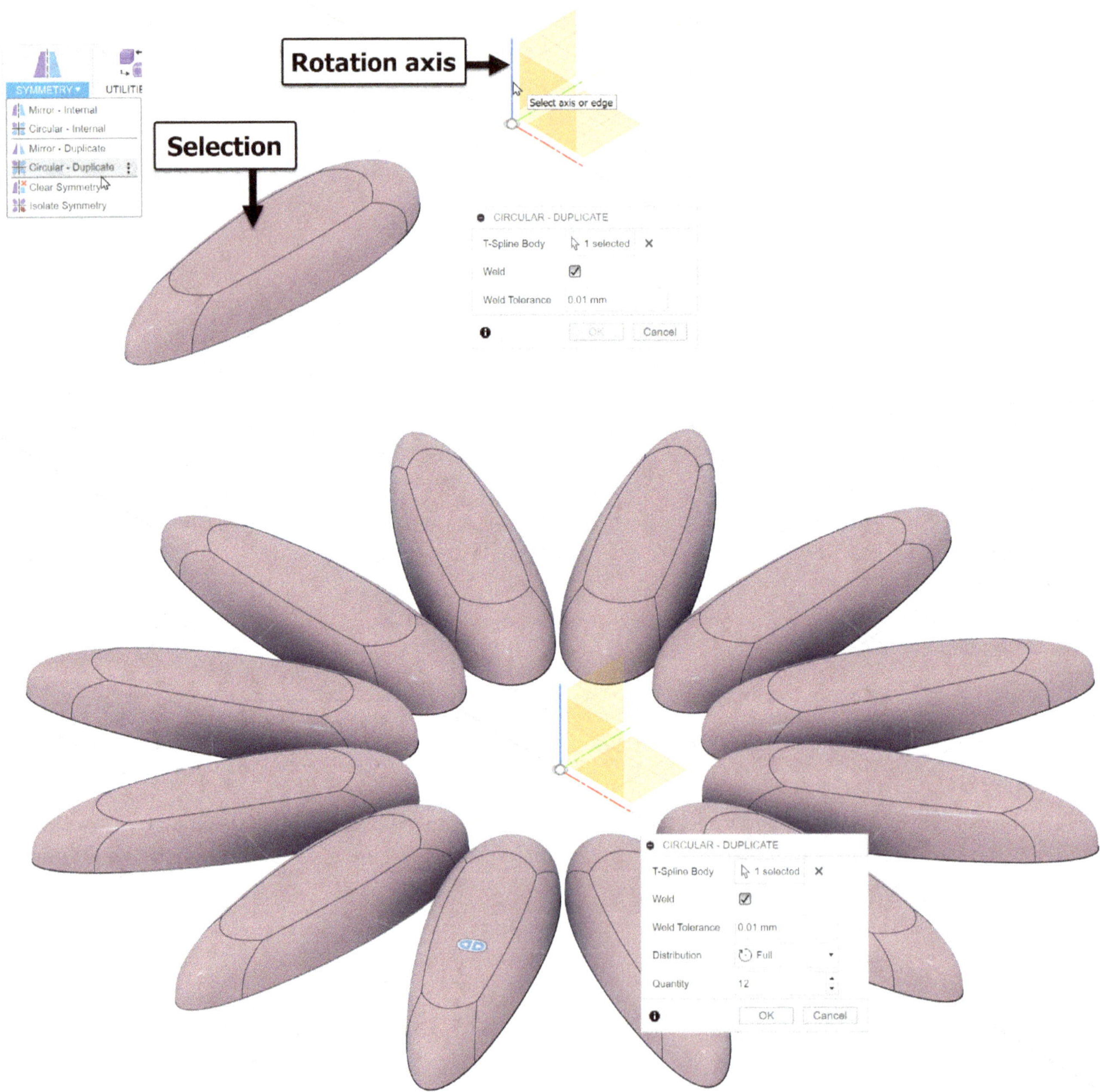

Mirror Duplicate

The **Mirror Duplicate** command helps you to allows you to mirror the selected T-spline body about a selected plane. Activate this command (on the toolbar, click **Form > Symmetry > Mirror Duplicate**) and select a face from the T-spline body. Next, select a plane about which the selected body is to be mirrored. Check the **Weld** option to weld the edges of the mirrored T-spline bodies. Note that the edges will be welded only if they are very near to each other. However, you can specify the **Weld tolerance** value to define the maximum allowable distance between edges for them to be welded together. Click **OK** to mirror the body.

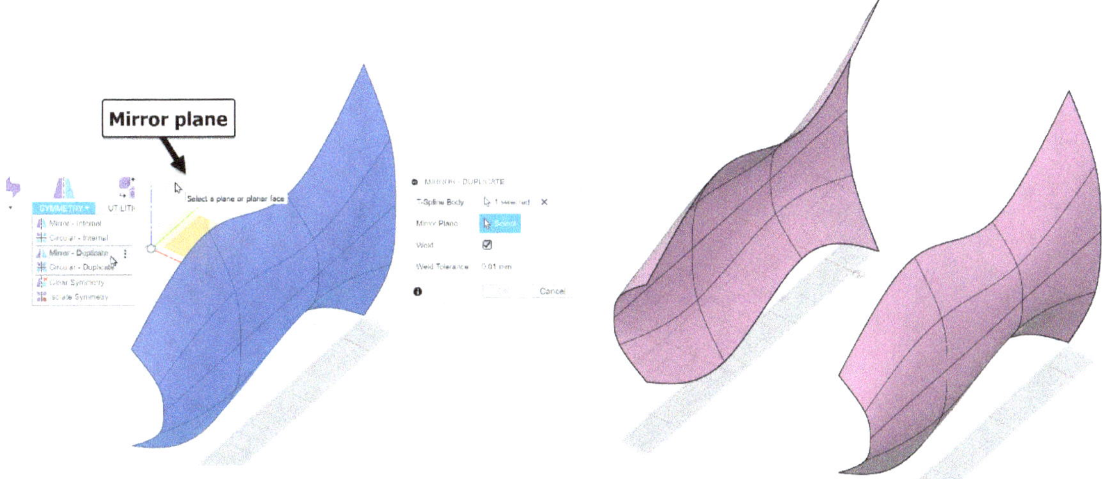

Cylindrify

The **Cylindrify** command cylindrifies an irregular surface. Activate this command (on the toolbar, click **Form >**

Modify > Cylindrify ) and select an uneven surface. Click **OK** on the **Cylindrify** dialog.

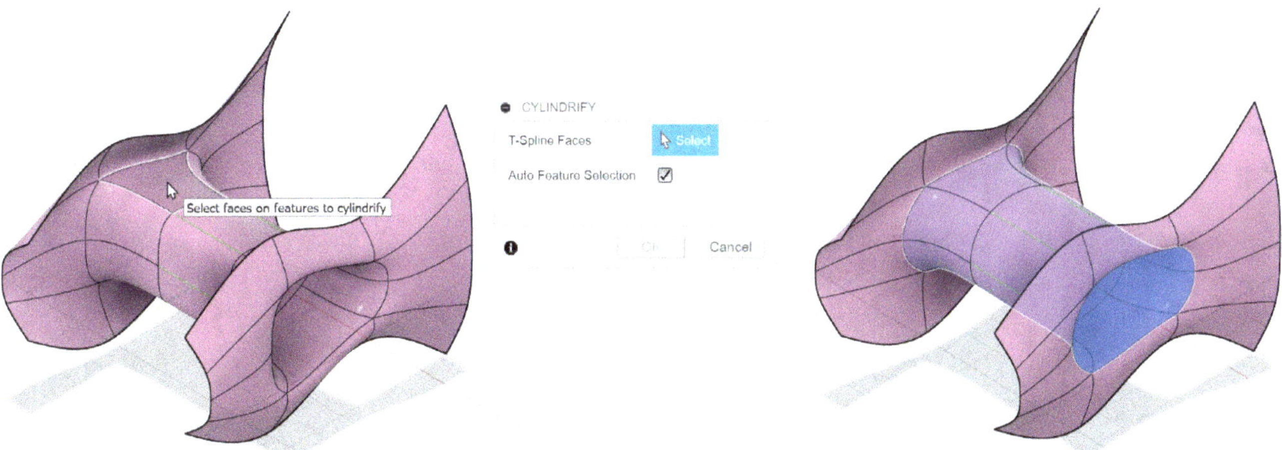

Filling the cage faces

The **Fill Hole** command adds a new face to the T-spline form using an edge of the opening. Activate this

command (on the toolbar, click **Create > Modify > Fill Hole**) and click on an edge of the opening. On the **Fill Hole** dialog, select an option from the **Fille Hole Mode** drop-down. The options (**Reduced Star, Fill Star, Collapse**) in this drop-down define how the edges are arranged on the fill surface.

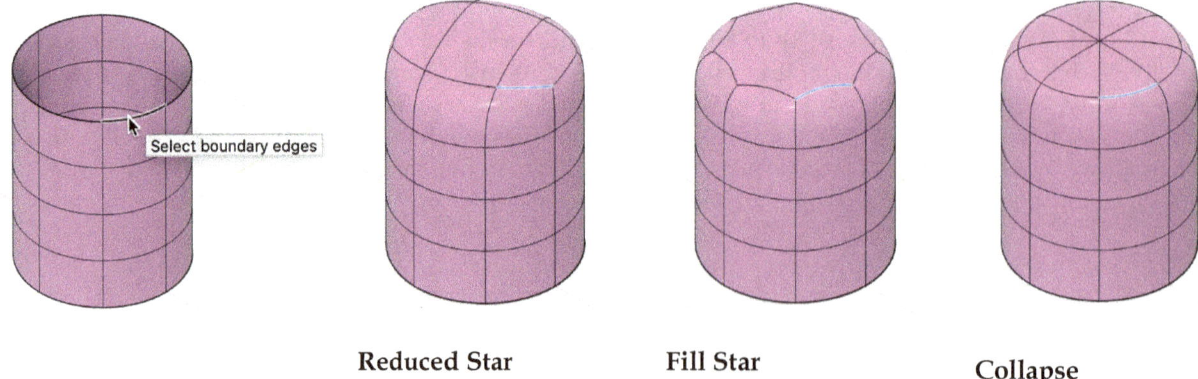

Check the **Keep Creases** option if you want to make the boundary edges of the hole sharp.

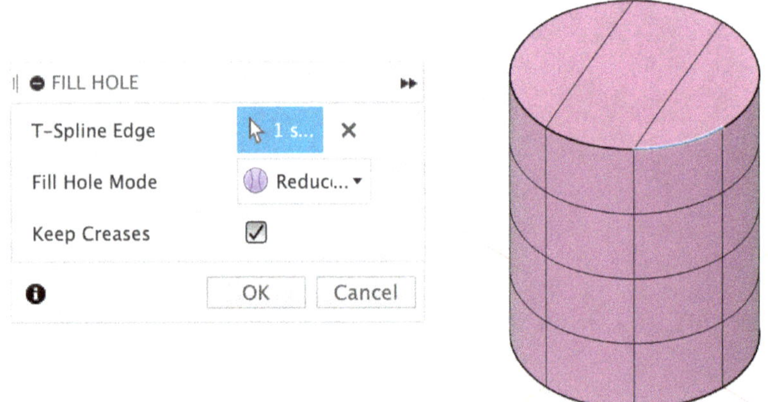

Erase and Fill

The **Erase and Fill** command erases and fills a selected face(s). Activate this command (on the toolbar, click **Form > Modify > Erase and Fill**) and select the face(s) to be erased. Next, select an option (**Reduced star** or **Fill star**)from the **Fill Hole mode** drop-down. Click **OK** on the **Erase and Fill** dialog.

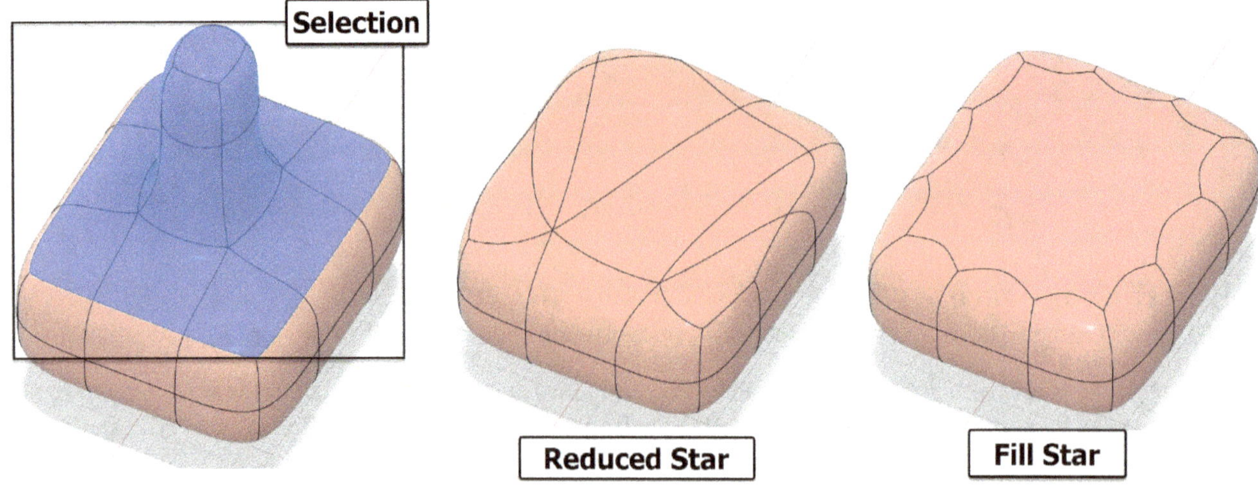

Weld Vertices

The **Weld Vertices** command is used to weld two vertices together. Activate this command (on the toolbar, click

Form > Modify > Weld Vertices) and select **Weld Mode > Vertex to Vertex** from the **Weld Vertices** dialog. Next, select the vertices to be welded and click **OK** on the **Weld Vertices** dialog.

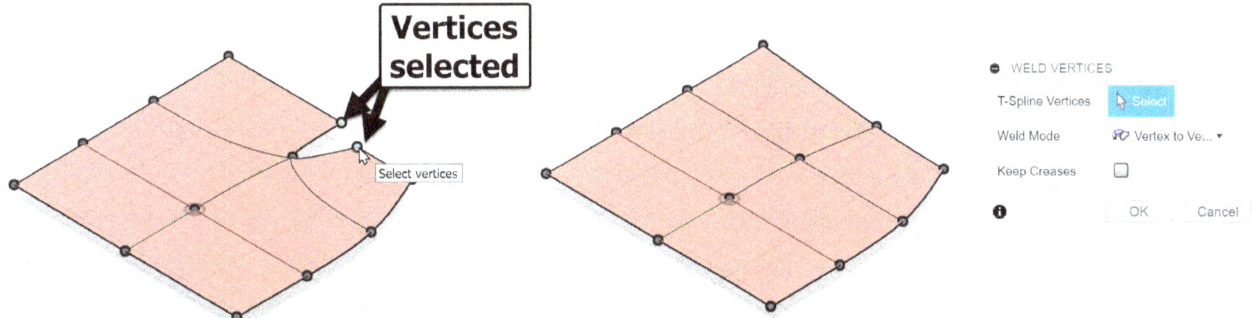

Unweld Edges

The **Unweld Edges** command split the T-spline body at the selected edge. Activate this command (on the toolbar, click **Form > Modify > Unweld Edges**) and double-click on an edge to select the edge loop. Next, click **OK** on the **Unweld Edges** dialog; the T-spline body is split. Next, activate the **Edit Form** command and double-click on the split portion; the split body is selected. Click and drag the arrow of the manipulator; the body is moved.

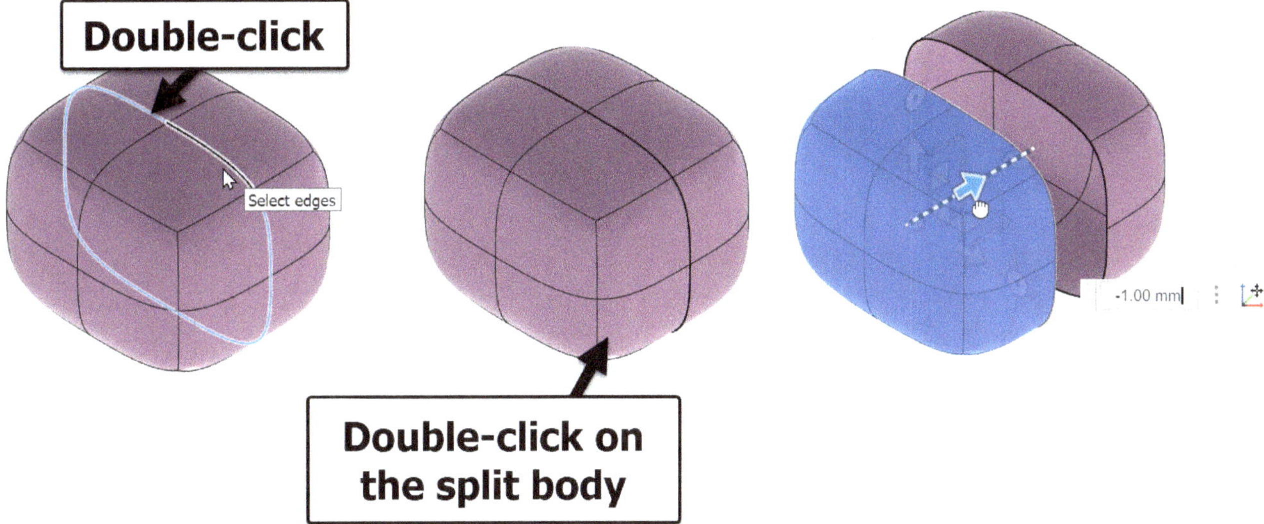

Subdivide

The **Subdivide** command splits a face into multiple faces uniformly or through selected points. The following example illustrates the use of this command. First, create a box with the specifications, as shown.

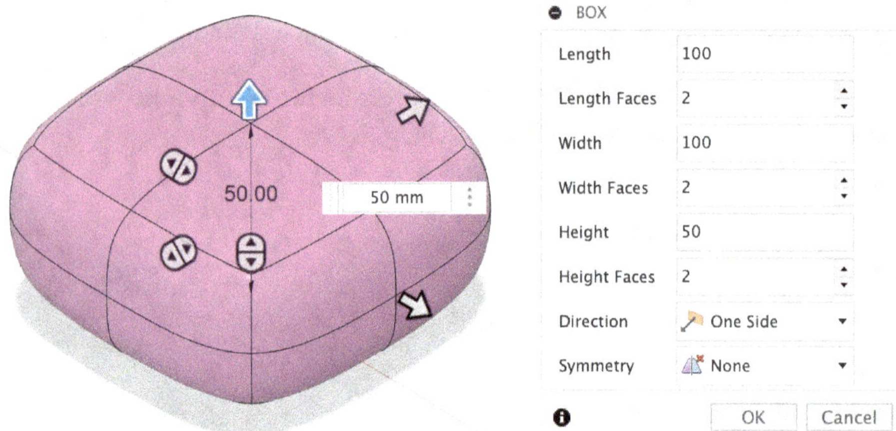

Activate the **Subdivide** command (on the toolbar, click **Form > Modify > Subdivide**), and then click on the face to split. Next, select **Insert Mode > Simple** from the **Subdivide** dialog; the subdivided face is flattened. Select Insert **Mode > Exact**; the subdivided face retains its original shape. Also, all the faces of the box are subdivided.

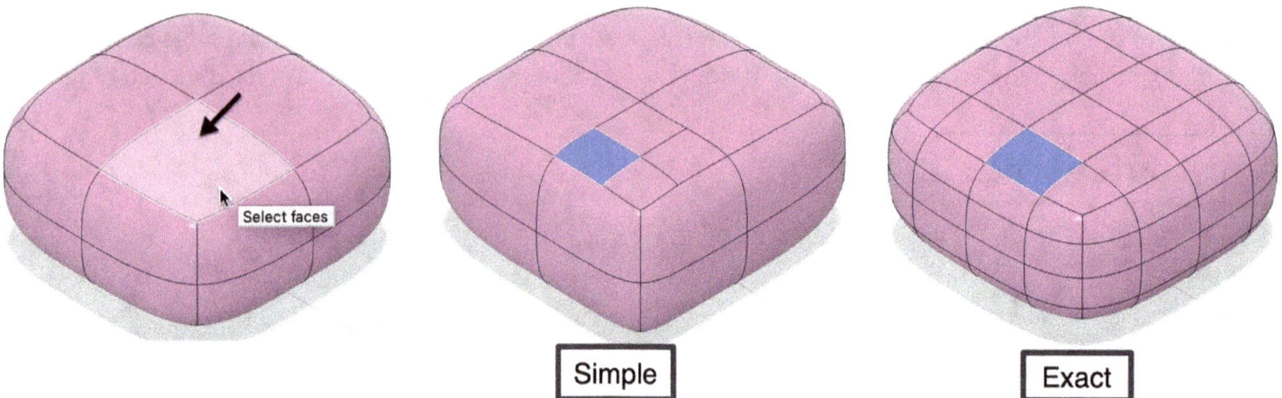

Check the **Specify** box and type-in values in the **Length Faces** and **Width Faces** box. Click OK to subdivide the selected face.

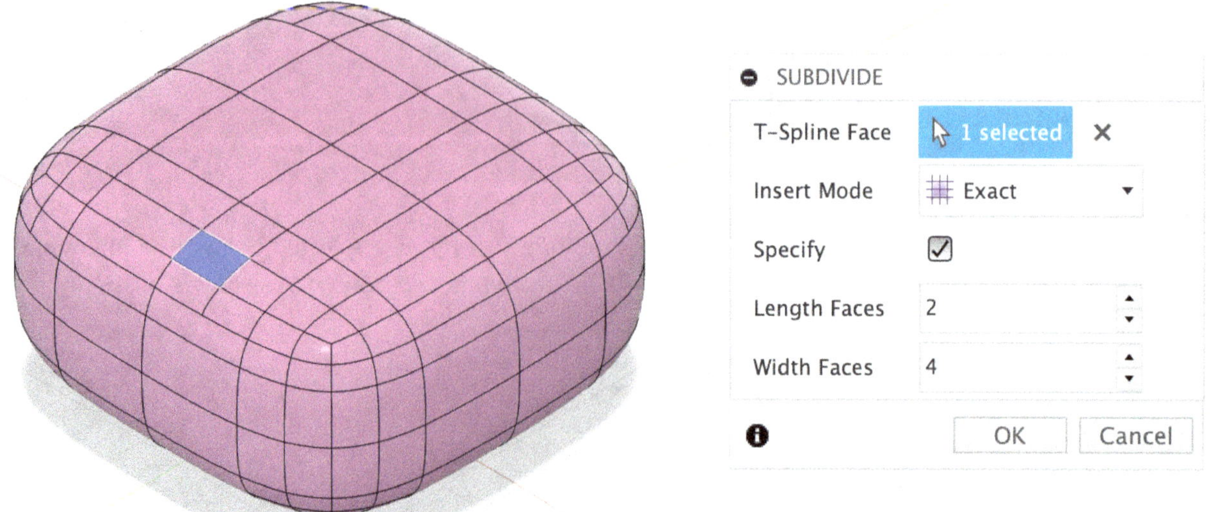

Crease

The **Crease** command allows you to sharpens the edges. For example, create a quadball with the **Span Faces** value of 1.

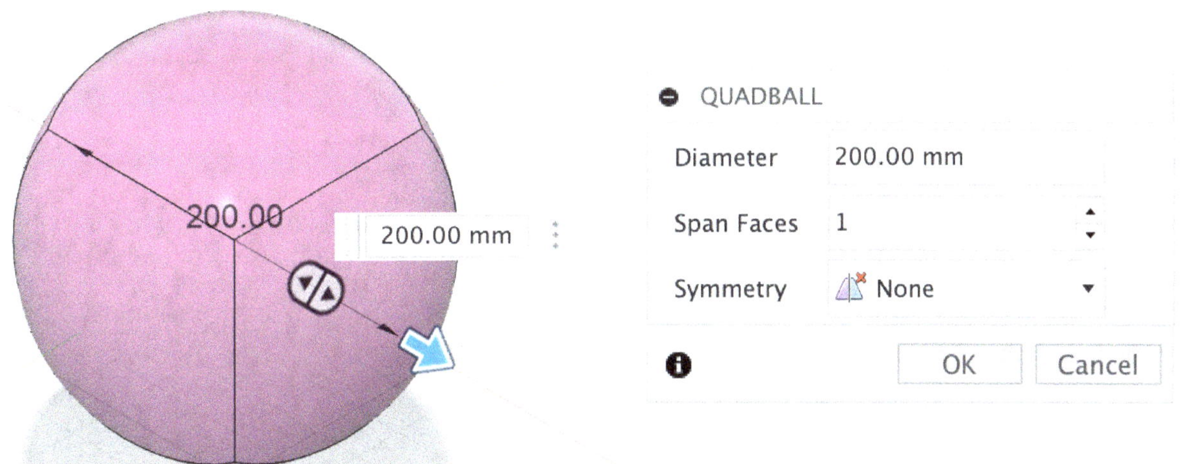

Click **Form > Modify > Crease** on the toolbar and select the top edges of the quadball. Click **OK** on the **Crease** dialog; the top edges of the quadball are sharpenned.

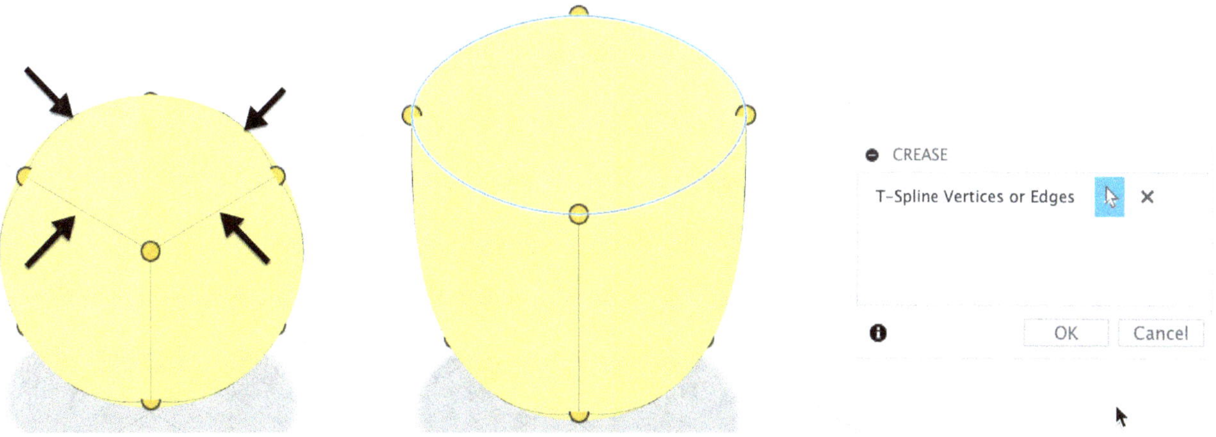

Bevel Edge

The **Bevel Edge** command remove a selected edge of a T-spline and add edges on its either side. On the toolbar, click **Form > Modify > Bevel Edge** and select the edge(s) from the T-spline. On the **Bevel Edge** dialog, specify the number of replacement edges in the **Segments** box. Next, use the **Bevel Location** box to specify the distance at which the replacement edges will be placed from the selected edge(s).

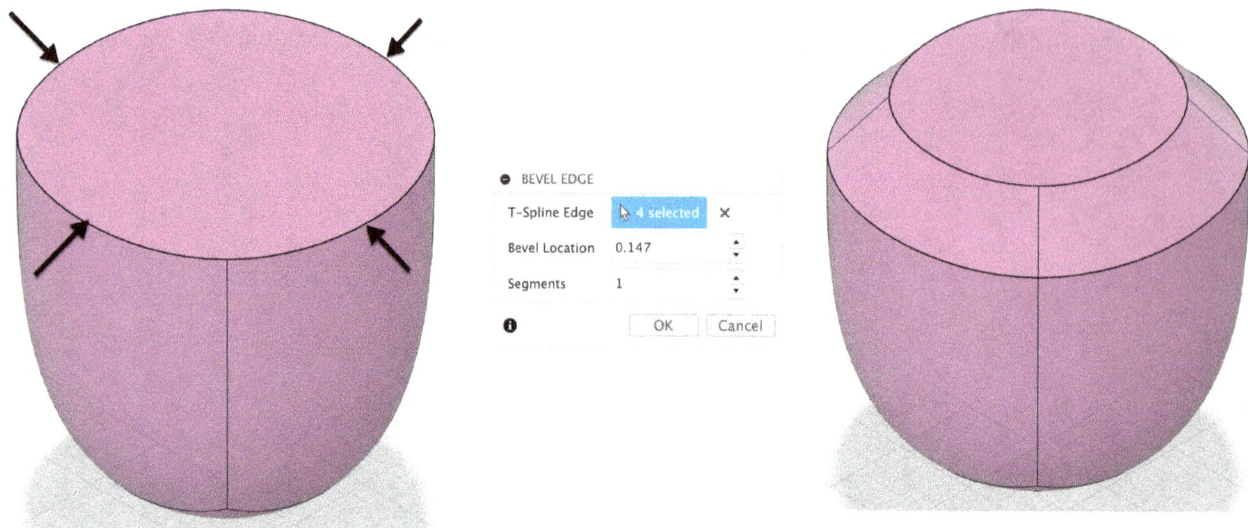

Uncrease

The **Uncrease** command smoothen the sharp edges. For example, Click **Form > Modify > Uncrease** on the toolbar and select the sharp edges, as shown. Next, click **OK** on the **Uncrease** dialog to smoothen the edges.

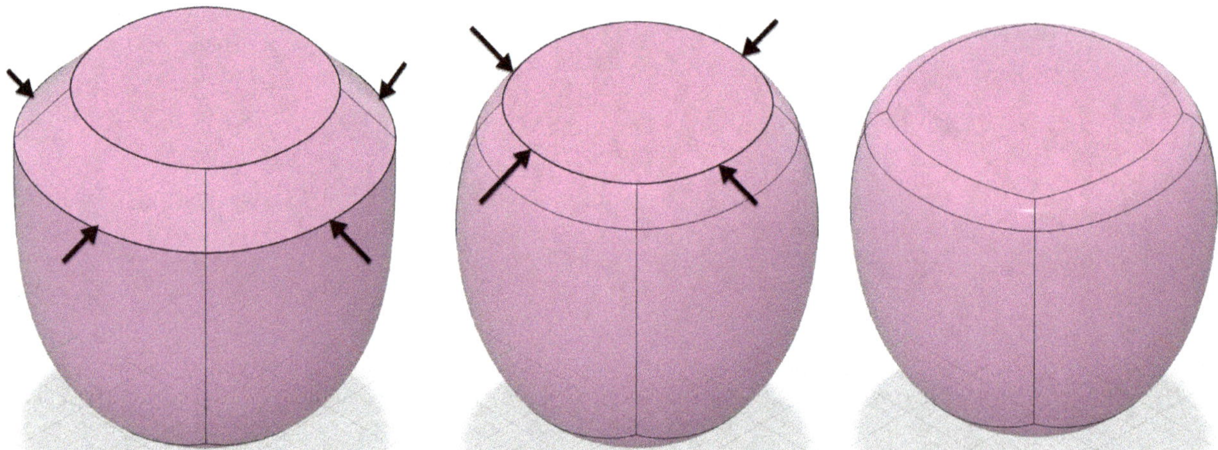

Insert Edges

The **Insert Edges** command helps you to add edges adjacent to a selected edge. You can insert edge on one side or both sides of the selected edge. Inserting edges will change the curvature of the surface at that particular location.

Activate this command (on the toolbar, click **Form > Modify > Insert Edge**) and select an edge from the T-spline surface. Next, select an option from the **Insertion slide** drop-down. The **Single** option inserts an edge on one side of the selected edge. The **Both** option inserts edges on both sides of the selected edge. Click and drag the handle displayed on the selected edge to specify the distance at which the new edge is to inserted. You can also enter a value in the **Insert Location** box available on the **Insert Edge** dialog.

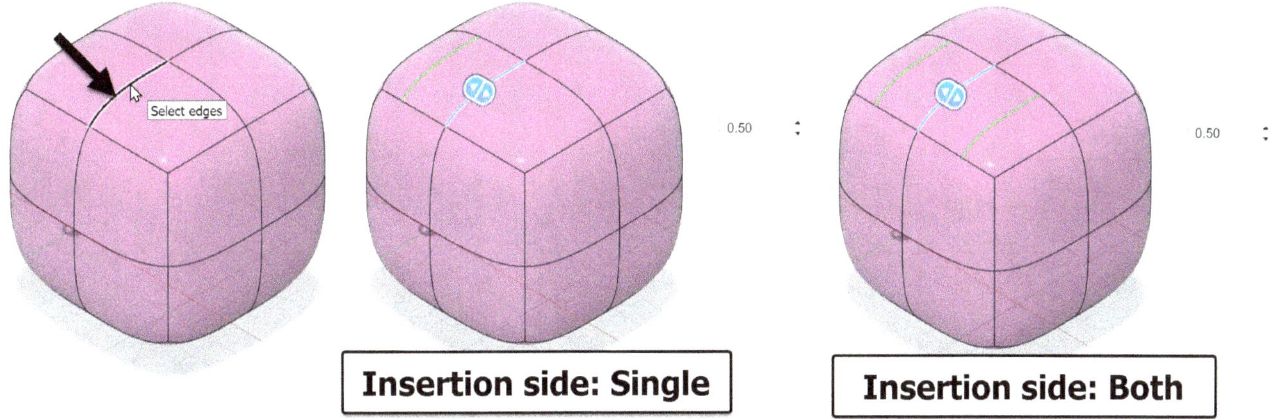

Select an option from the **Insertion Mode** drop-down. The **Simple** option inserts a simple on adjacent to the selected edge.

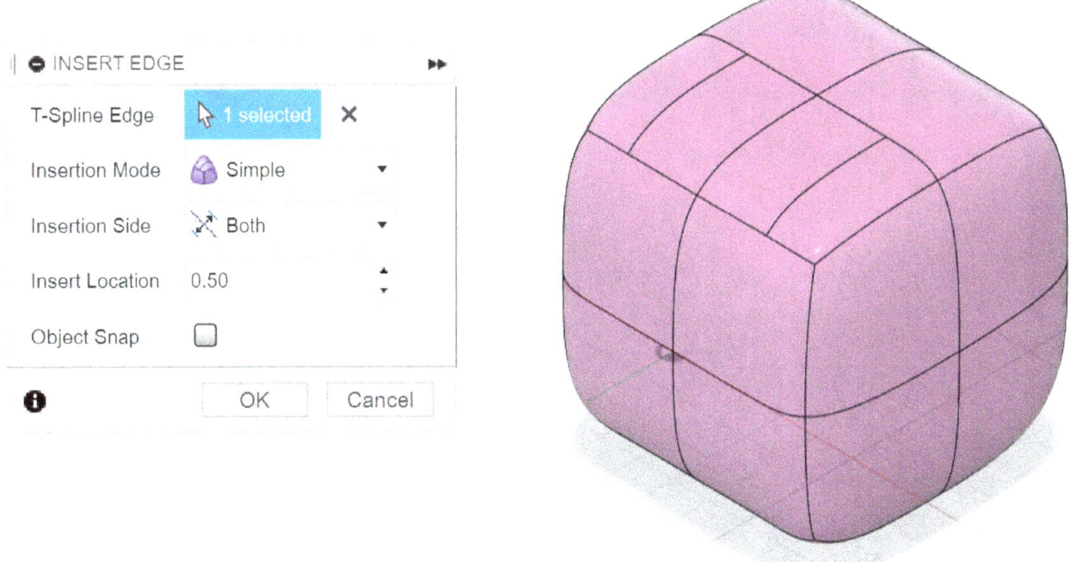

On the toolbar, click **Form > Modify > Edit Form** and select the face of the T-spline, as shown. Press and hold the left mouse button on the arrow pointing upwards, and then drag up to a small distance and click. Click **OK** on the **Edit Form** dialog; the T-spline surface is modified, as shown.

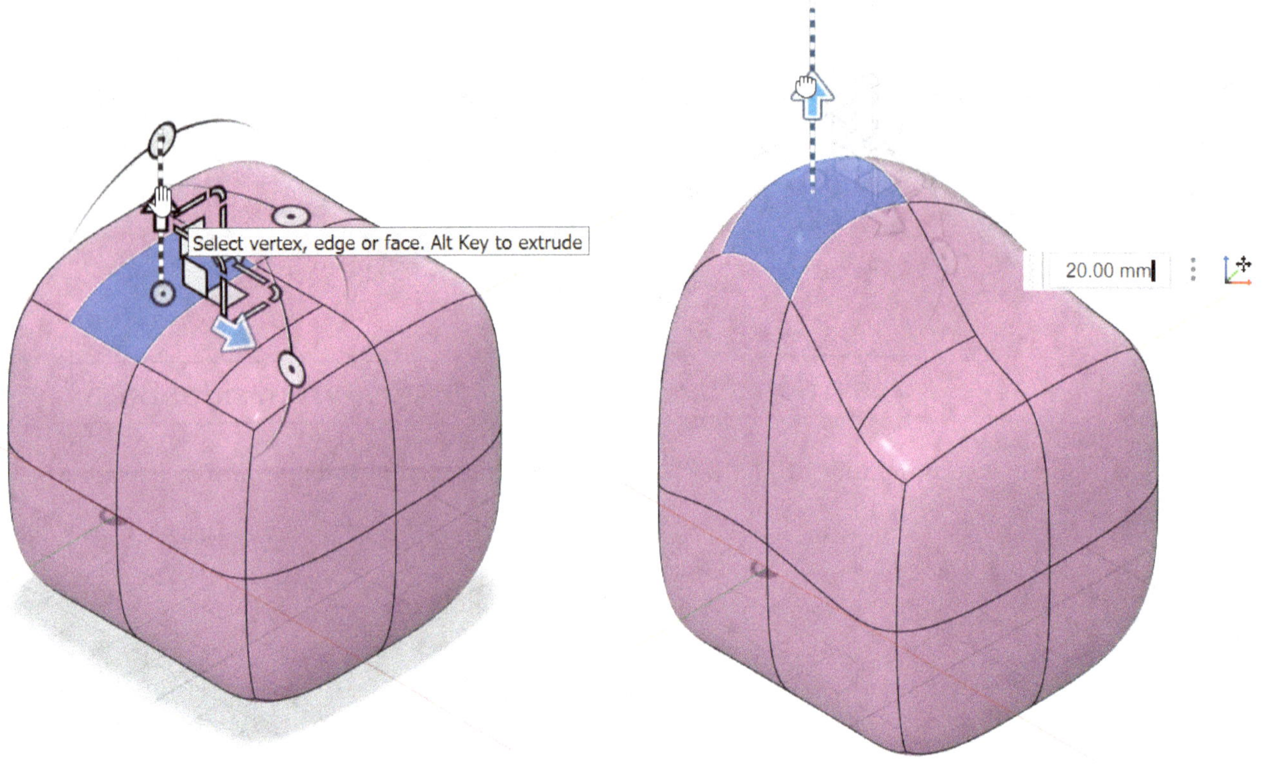

Double-click on the edge, as shown. The entire edge loop is selected.

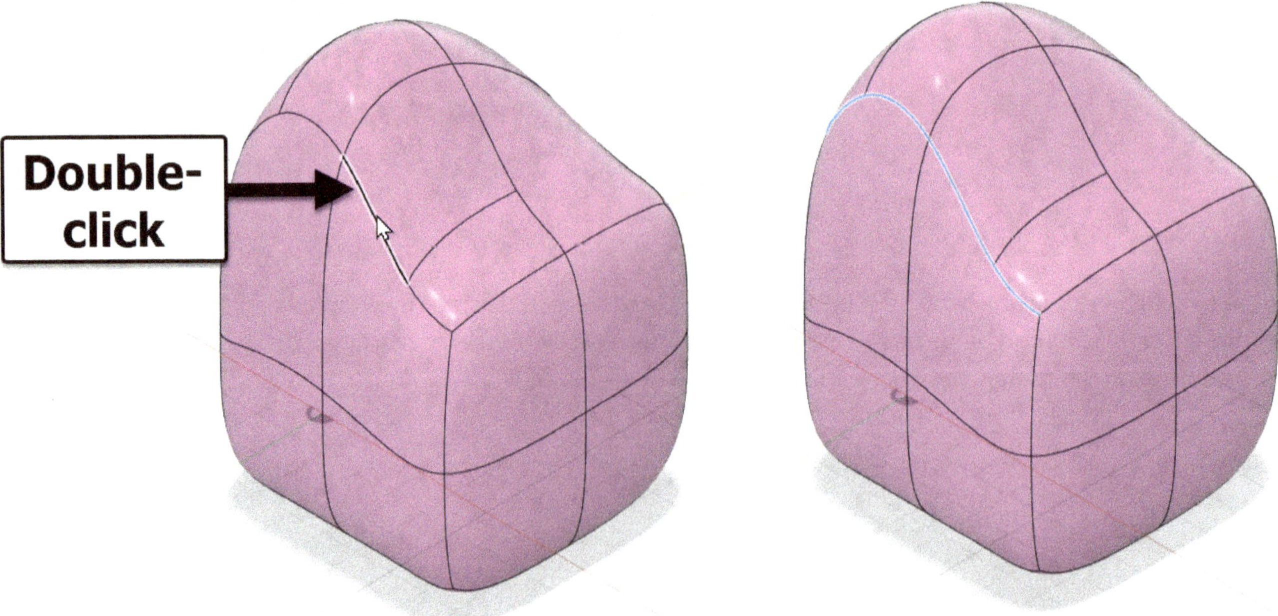

On the toolbar, click **Form > Modify > Insert Edge**. Next, select **Insertion Mode > Simple** and **Insertion side > Both.** Next, click and drag the handle displayed on the selected edge to specify the location of the new edges. Click **OK** and notice that the shape of the T-spline surface is changed.

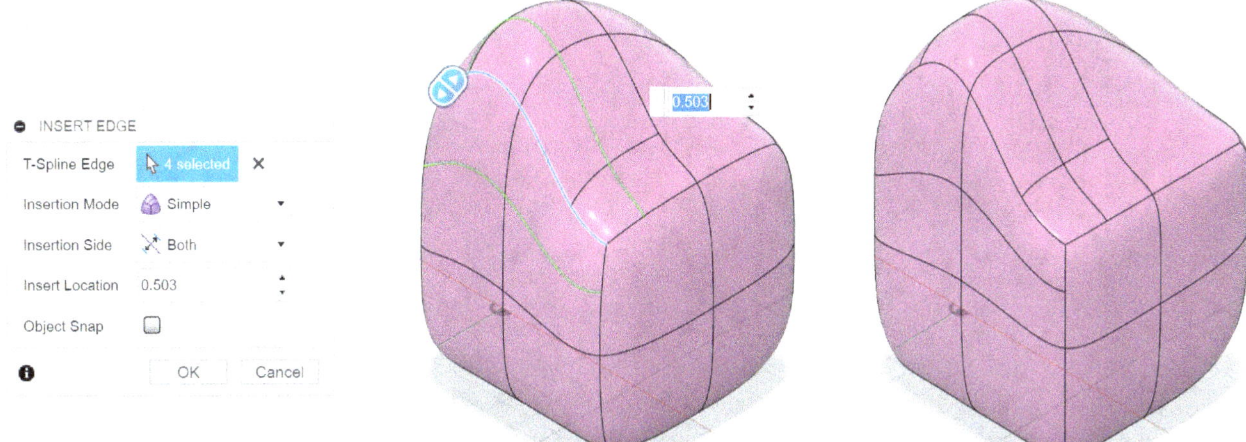

Press the CTRL+Z key on your keyboard or click the **Undo** icon on the Application Bar. Next, double-click on the curved edge, as shown. On the toolbar, click **Form > Modify > Insert Edge**. Next, select **Insertion Mode > Exact.** Click and drag the handle displayed on the selected edge to specify the location of the new edge. Click **OK** on the **Insert Edge** dialog and notice that the edges are added to all the faces of the T-spline surface. It helps you to keep the shape of the T-spline intact.

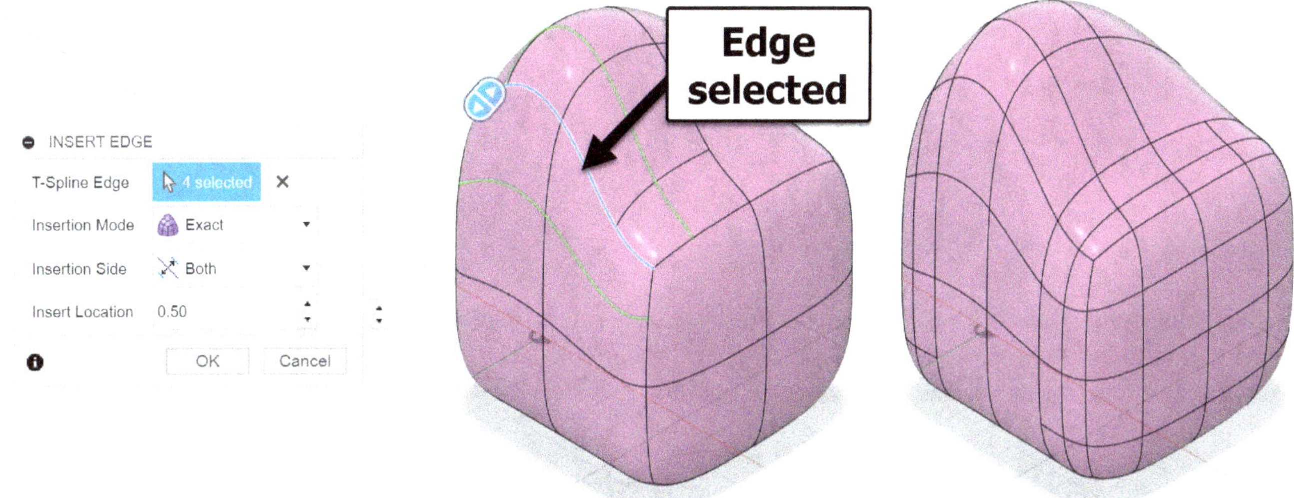

Insert Points

The **Insert Points** command helps you to add edges to the faces of the T-spline surface by selecting points. This command helps you to add individual edges that can be parallel or non-parallel to the adjacent edges. For

example, create a box , as shown in the figure below. Next, click **Form > Create > Extrude** on the toolbar and select the face of the box, as shown. Click and drag the arrow displayed on the selected face up to a small distance. Next, click **OK** on the **Extrude** dialog.

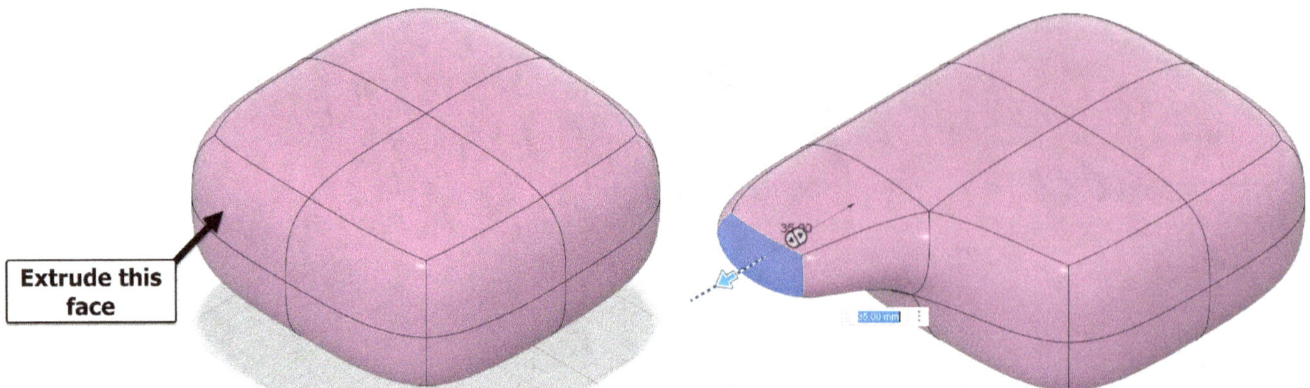

Double-click on the middle edge of the box to select the edge loop. Next, click **Form > Modify > Insert Edge**. Next, insert edges on both sides of the selected edge and click **OK**. Notice that the inserted edges do not extend up to the extruded portion.

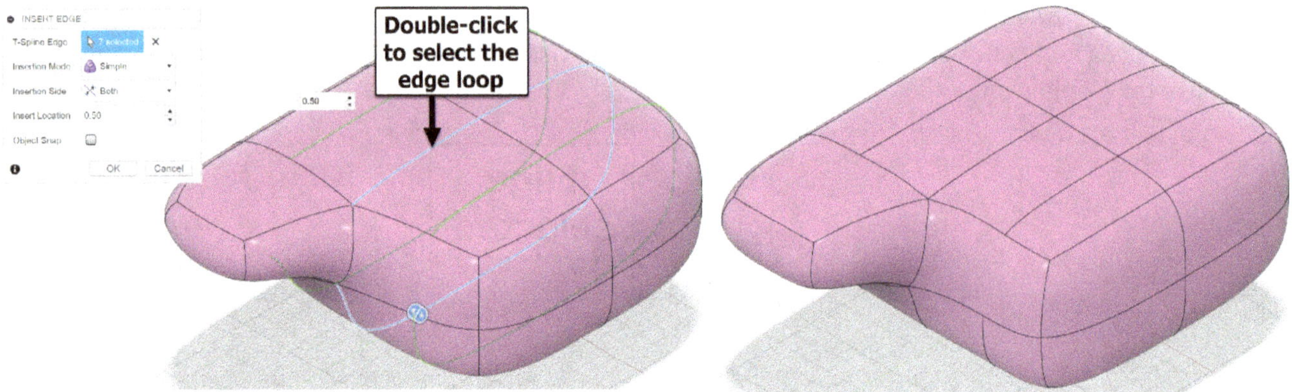

On the toolbar, click **Form > Modify > Insert Point** . Next, select **Insertion Mode > Simple** from the **Insert Points** dialog. Select the points from the T-spline edges, as shown. An edge is added connecting the two points. Likewise, continue to select points from the edges, as shown. Next, click **OK** to insert edges.

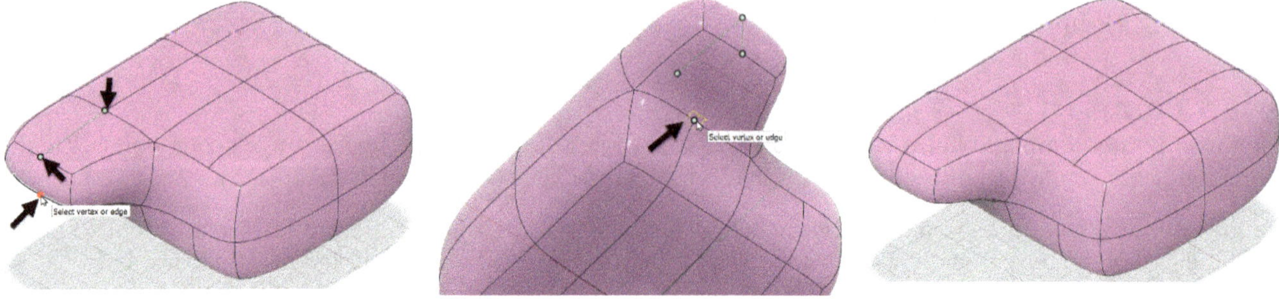

Click the **Undo** icon on the Application Bar. Click **Form > Modify > Insert Point** on the toolbar. Next, select **Insertion Mode > Exact** from the **Insert Point** dialog. Select the midpoint of the edge, as shown. Click **OK** on the dialog and notice that an edge is added passing through the selected point. Also, similar edges are added to the other faces.

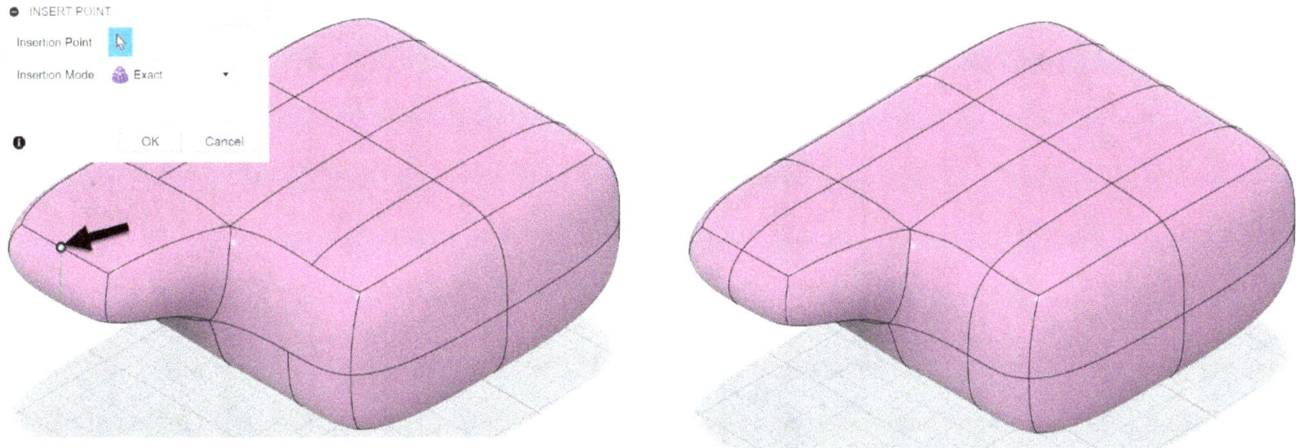

Slide Edge

The **Slid Edge** command helps you to smoothen or sharpen the T-spline surfaces by moving sliding the edges. The distance between two edges defines the smoothness of a T-spline surface. The edges that are closer together harden the T-spline surface. For example, double-click on the edge, as shown in figure. The edge loop is selected.

Next, click **Form > Modify > Slide Edge** on the toolbar. Click and drag the handle displayed on the selected edge toward right. Next, specify the **Slide Location** value on the **Slide Edge** dialog and click **OK**. Notice that the T-spline edge is hardened.

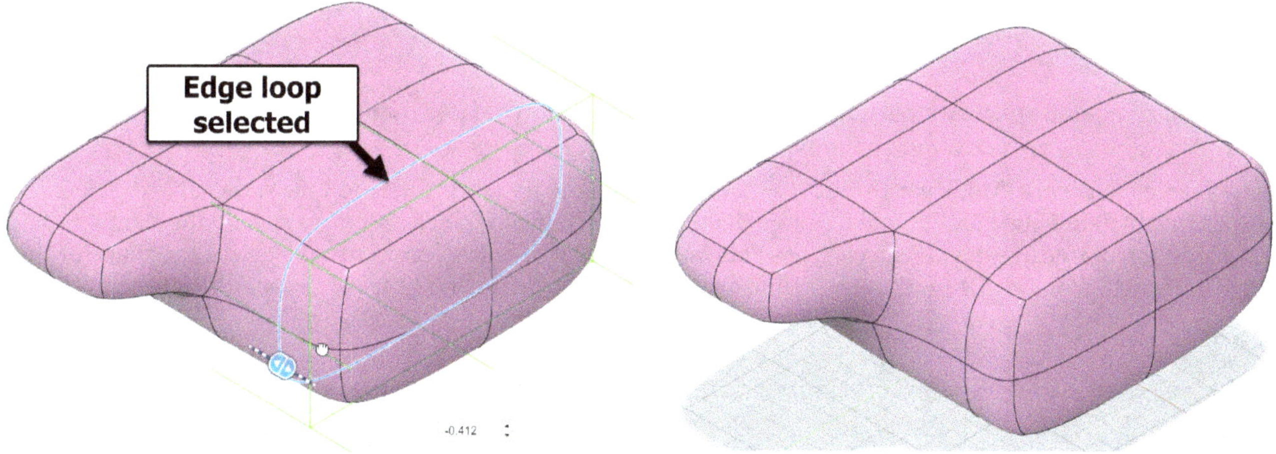

Merge Edge

The **Merge Edge** command merges two edges or edge loops. On the toolbar, click **Form > Modify > Merge Edge**. Select a single edge or edge loop (double-click on an edge to select the edge loop). On the **Merge Edge** dialog, click the **Edge Group Two** select button and select the second edge or group of edges. Next, click **OK** to merge the selected edges.

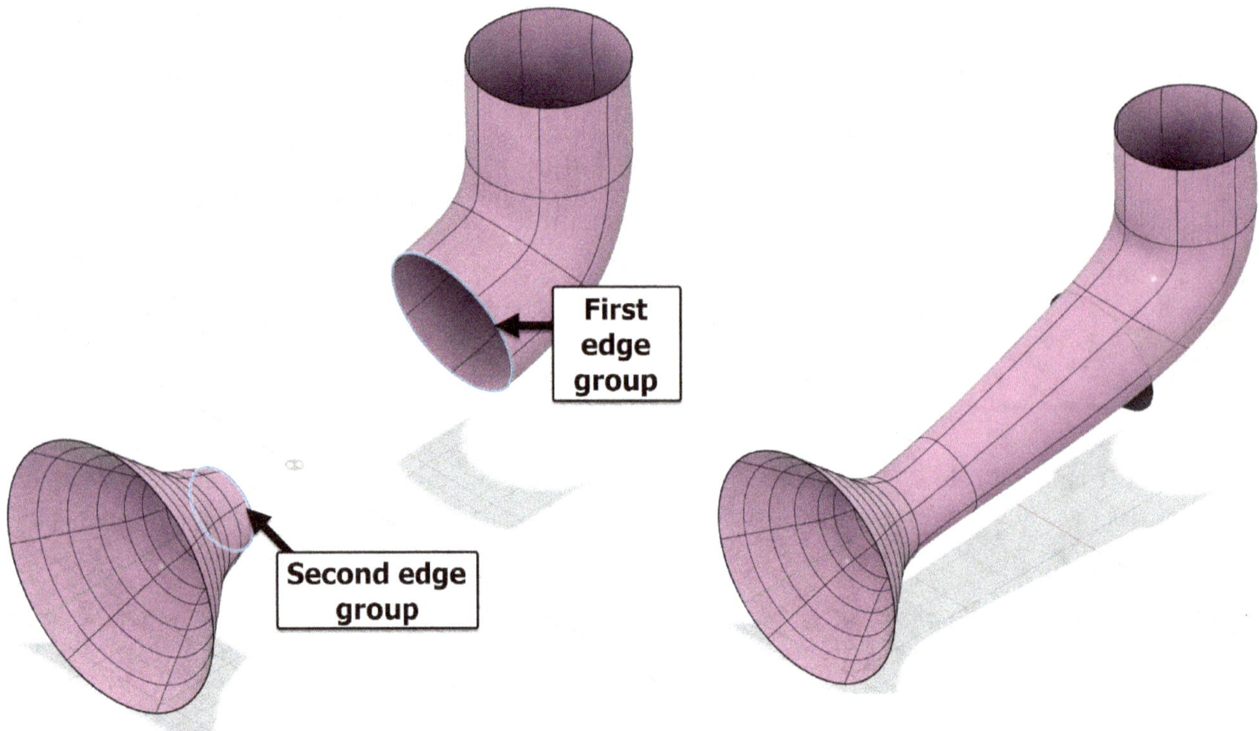

Bridge

The **Bridge** command creates a closed tunnel-like surface between two faces. Activate the **Bridge** command (on the toolbar, click **Form > Modify > Bridge**) and select a face to define the Side 1, as shown. Next, select another face to define the Side 2. On the Bridge dialog, enter a value in the **Faces** box to specify the number of faces along the bridge. Next, you can click the **Follow Curve** button and select a curve to define the shape of the bridge. However, you can **OK** without selecting a shape curve to create bridge face between the selected faces.

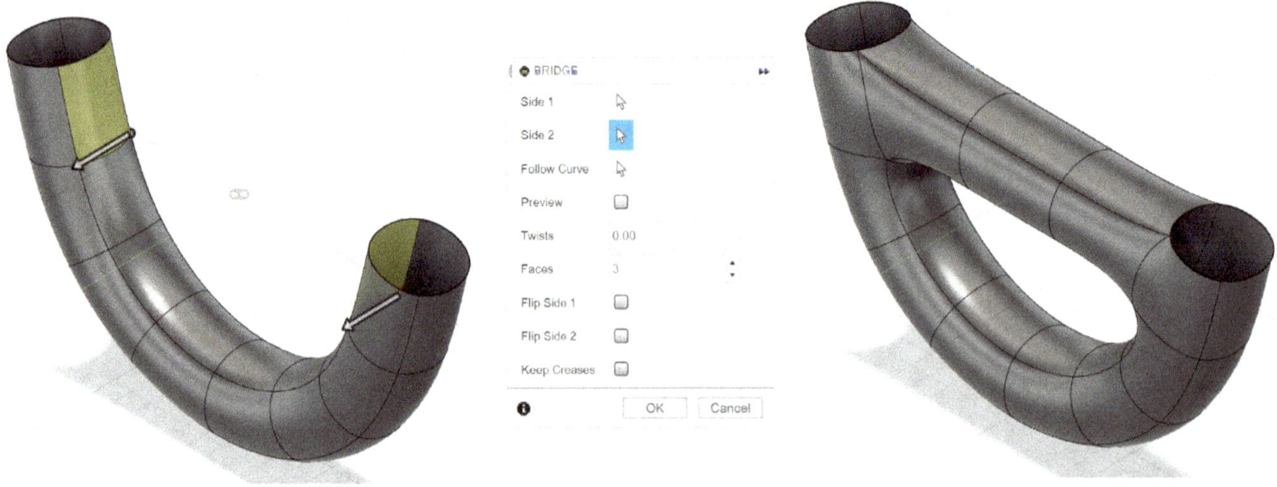

Match

The **Match** command aligns the edges of a T-spline surface to a selected curve. For example, create a box and the curve, as shown. Next, activate this command (on the toolbar, click **Form > Modify > Match**). Next, select the T-spline edges, as shown. Click the **Match Edges** selection button and select the curve to which the T-spline edges are to be matched.

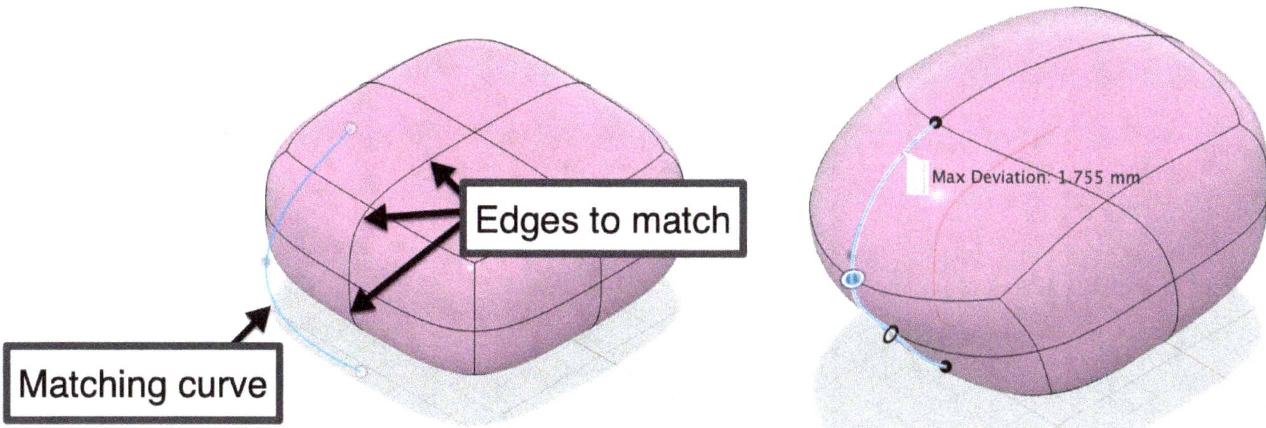

You can specify the spacing between the edges normal to the selected edges using the Spacing drop-down. The **Uniform** option creates a uniform spacing between the edges. The **Curvature** option varies the spacing between the edges based on the curvature of the matching curve. Next, click **OK** on the **Match** dialog.

Associative Match

The **Associative** option allows you to match the edges of a T-spline surface to a parametric sketch or edges of a parametric geometry. For example, you can match the edges of the T-spline cylinder to a parametric sketch created outside the Form environment. To do this, click **Form > Modify > Match** on the toolbar and check the Associative option on the **Match** dialog. Next, select the bottom edges of the cylinder. Click the Matched Edges selection button on the **Match** dialog and select the sketch; the bottom edges of the cylinder are matched to the selected sketch.

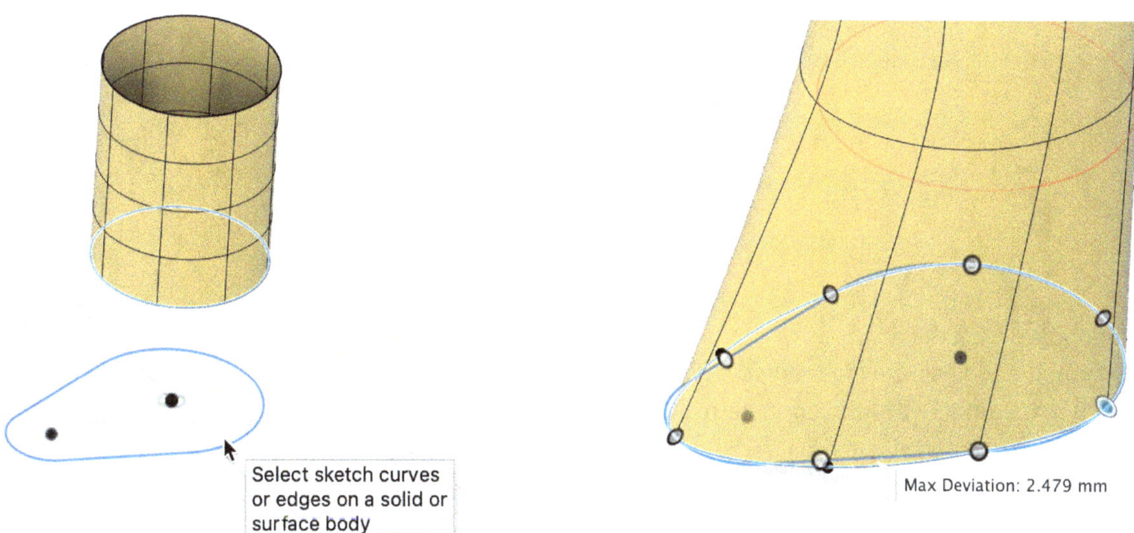

Notice that the vertices of the T-spline edges does not match with that of the sketch. On the **Match** dialog, check the **Tolerance** option, and then enter **0.5** in the **Edge Tolerance** box; the vertices of the cylinder edge are matched to that of the sketch. Click **OK** on the **Match** dialog.

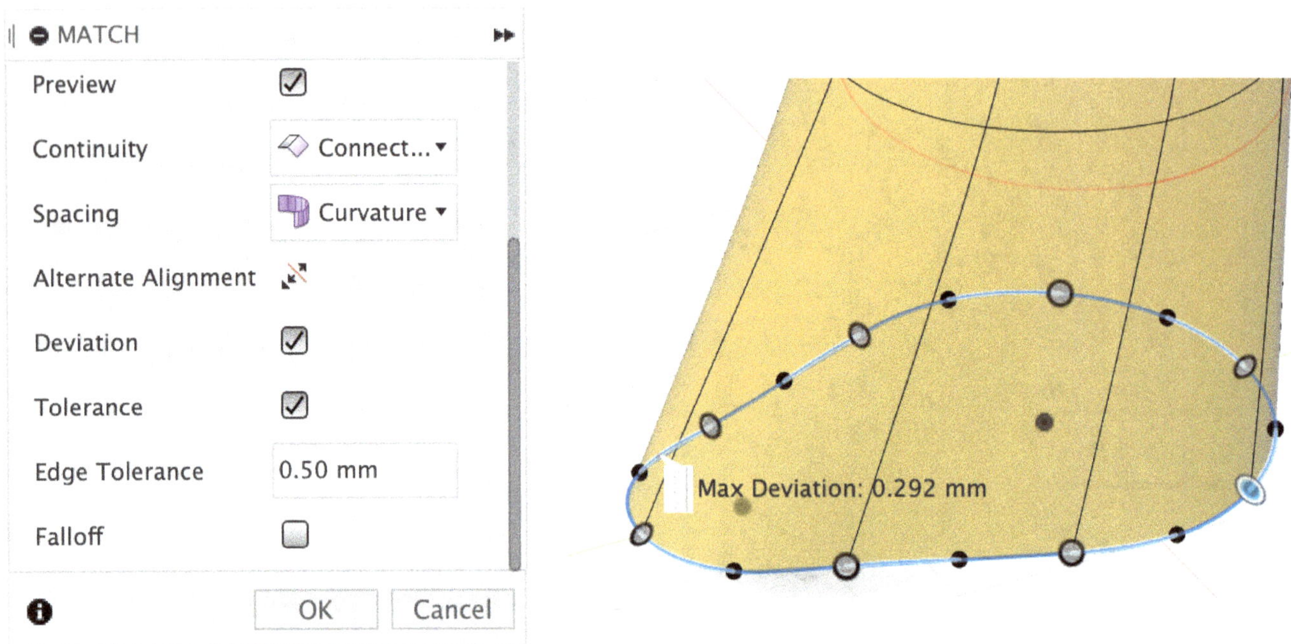

Click **Finish Form** on the toolbar, right-click on the **Sketch** in the **Browser** and select **Edit Sketch**. Next, modify the sketch and click the **Finish Sketch** on the toolbar. Notice that the T-spline surface is updated to match the edited sketch.

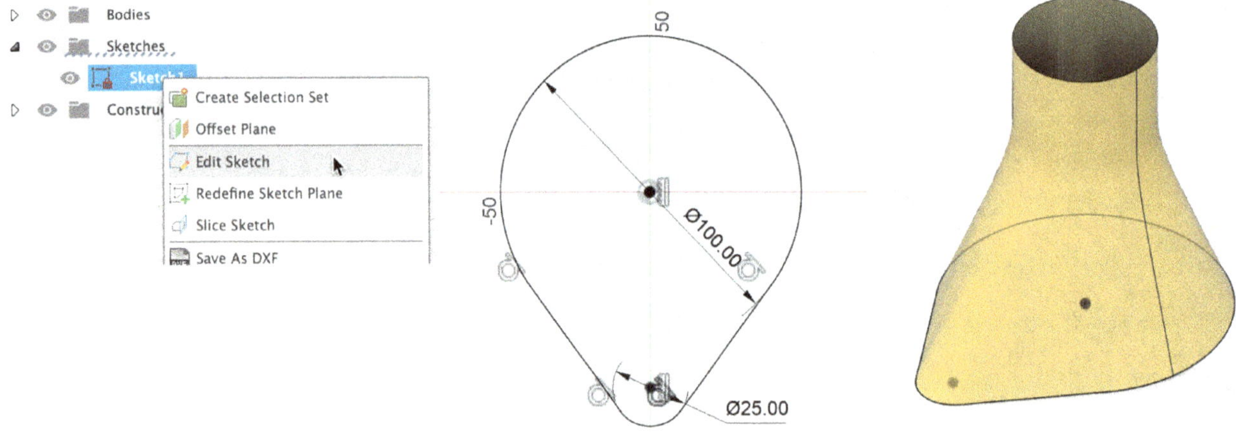

On the Application Bar, click the down-arrow next to the **Undo** icon and select **Undo Create Form**. Next, click the **Finish Form** icon on the toolbar. On the toolbar, click **Surface > Create > Extrude** and select the sketch. Next, extrude the sketch in the downward direction with a taper of 15 degrees.

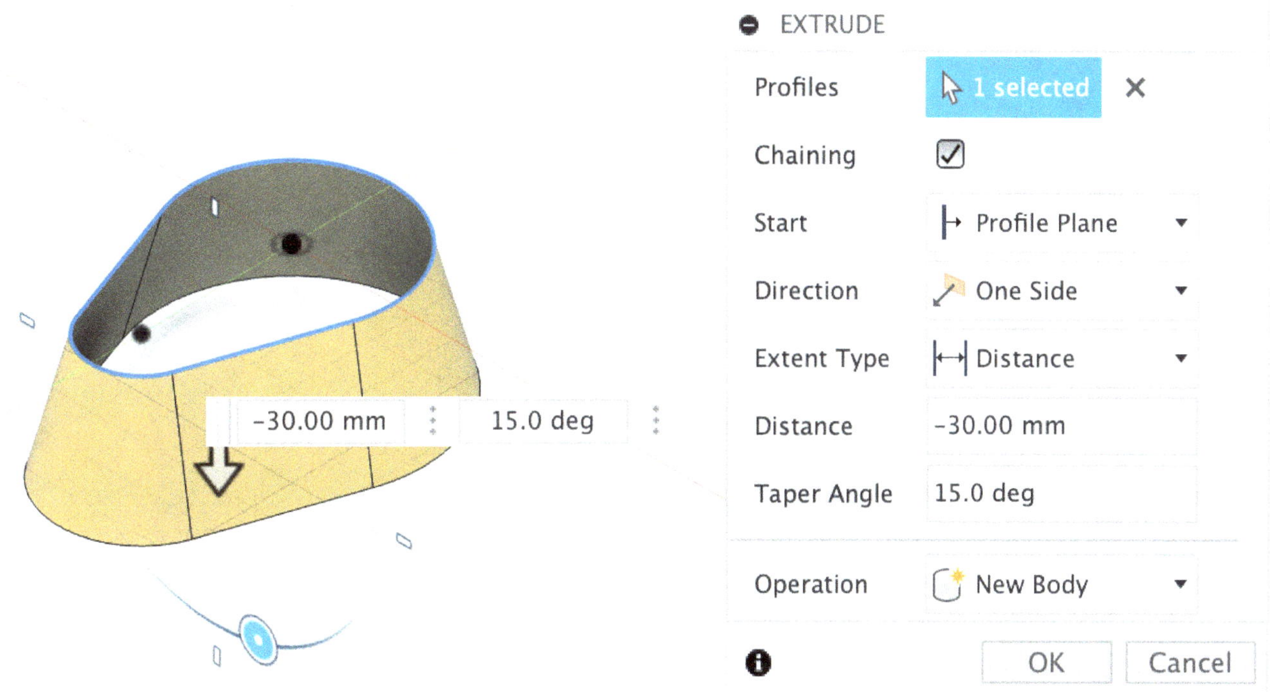

In the toolbar, click on the **Create Form** icon on the **Surface** tab. Next, create a offset plane, as shown.

Create a Cylinder on the newly created offset plane, as shown. On the toolbar, click **Form > Modify > Match** and check the **Associative** option. Select the bottom edges of the cylinder and click the **Match Edges** selection button. Select the top edge of the extruded surface.

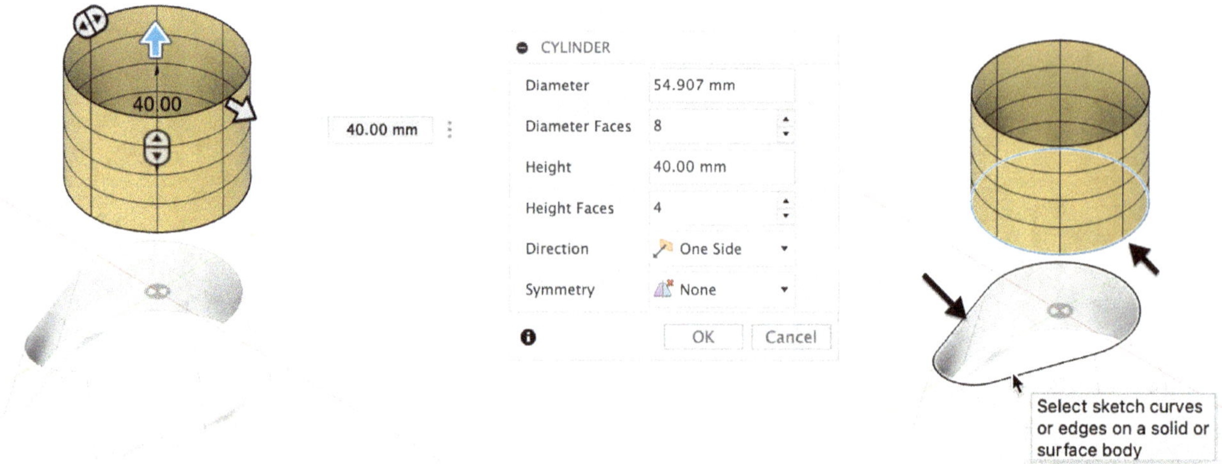

Select **Continuity > Tangent (G1)** to make the T-spline tangent to the matched surface. You can also select **Continuity > Curvature** if you want to make the T-spline curvature continuous with matched surface.

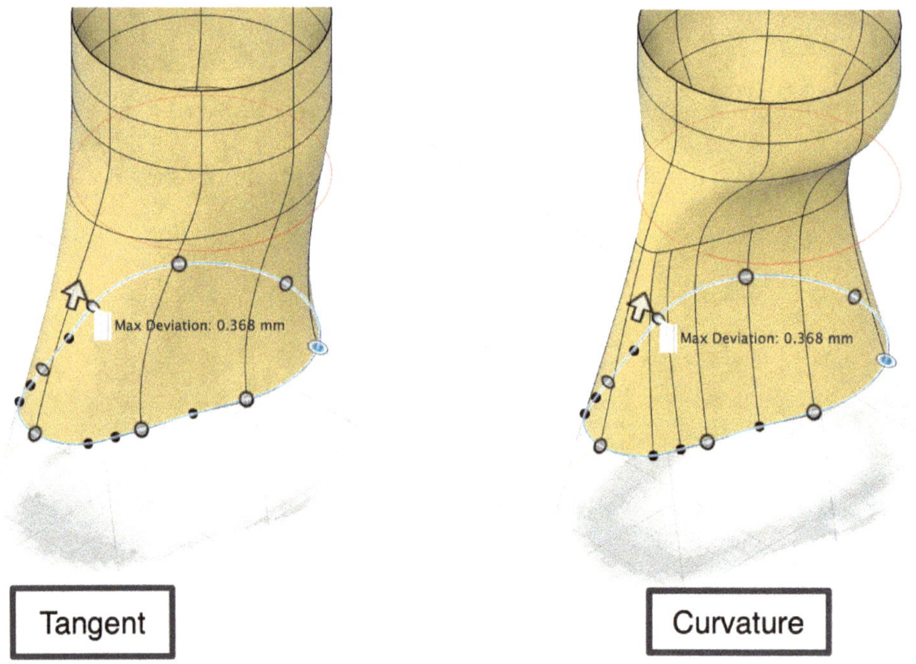

Notice that select Curvature (G1) continuity results in a botched T-spline surface. However, you can rectify this up to using the **Falloff** option. Check the **Falloff** option on the Match dialog and specify the **Falloff Distance** value. You can also click and drag the arrow displayed on the T-spline surface to adjust the Falloff Distance. The Falloff Distance defines the extent up to which the T-spline surface is influenced from the matched surface.

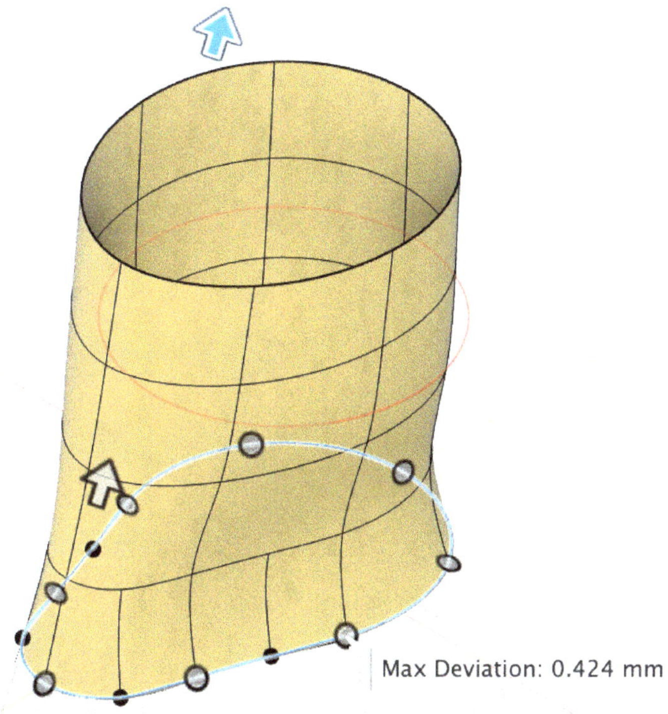

Max Deviation: 0.424 mm

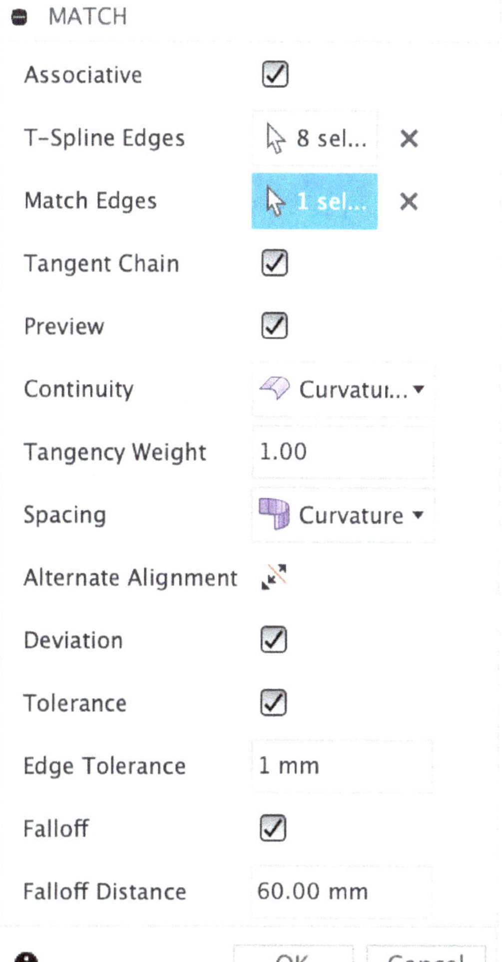

MATCH
Associative
T-Spline Edges   8 sel...
Match Edges   1 sel...
Tangent Chain
Preview
Continuity   Curvatur...
Tangency Weight   1.00
Spacing   Curvature
Alternate Alignment
Deviation
Tolerance
Edge Tolerance   1 mm
Falloff
Falloff Distance   60.00 mm
OK   Cancel

Example 1

In this example, you will construct the model shown below.

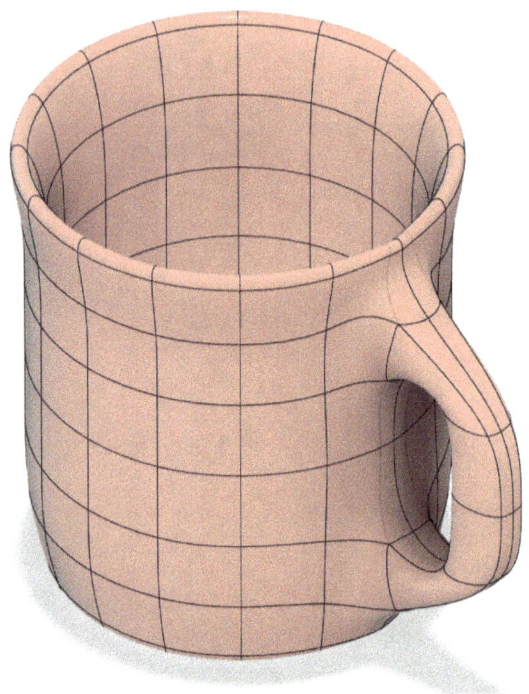

Activating the Form Workspace

1. Start **Autodesk Fusion 360** and start a new design file.

2. On the toolbar, click **Solid > Create > Create Form**.

Creating a Cylinder Form

1. On the toolbar, click **Form > Create > Cylinder**. Next, select the **Symmetric** option from the **Direction** drop-down available on the **Cylinder** dialog.
2. Select the origin point from the graphics window. Next, move the pointer outward and click.

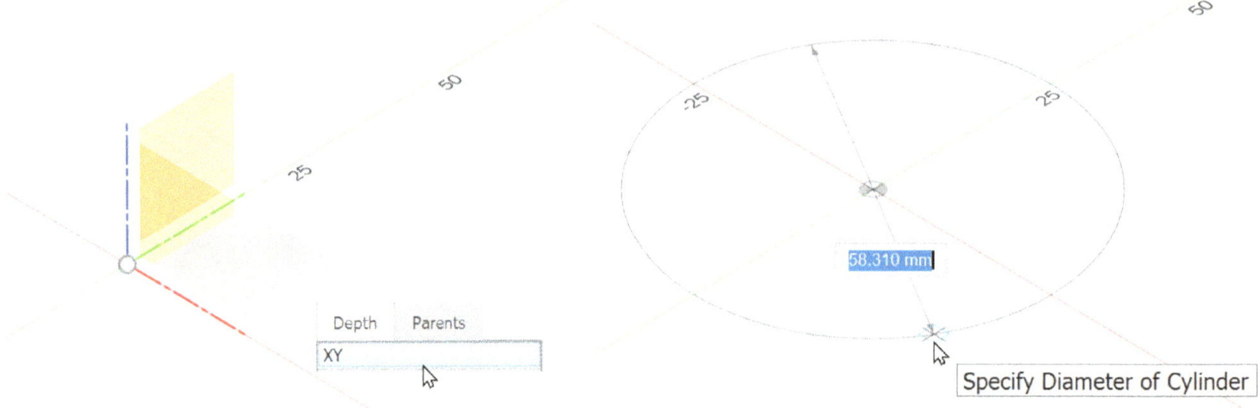

3. On the Cylinder dialog, type **80** and **90** in the **Diameter** and **Height** boxes, respectively. Next, type 16 and 6 in the **Diameter Faces** and **Height Faces** boxes of the **Cylinder** dialog.

4. On the **Cylinder** dialog, select **Symmetry > None** and click **OK** to create the cylinder.

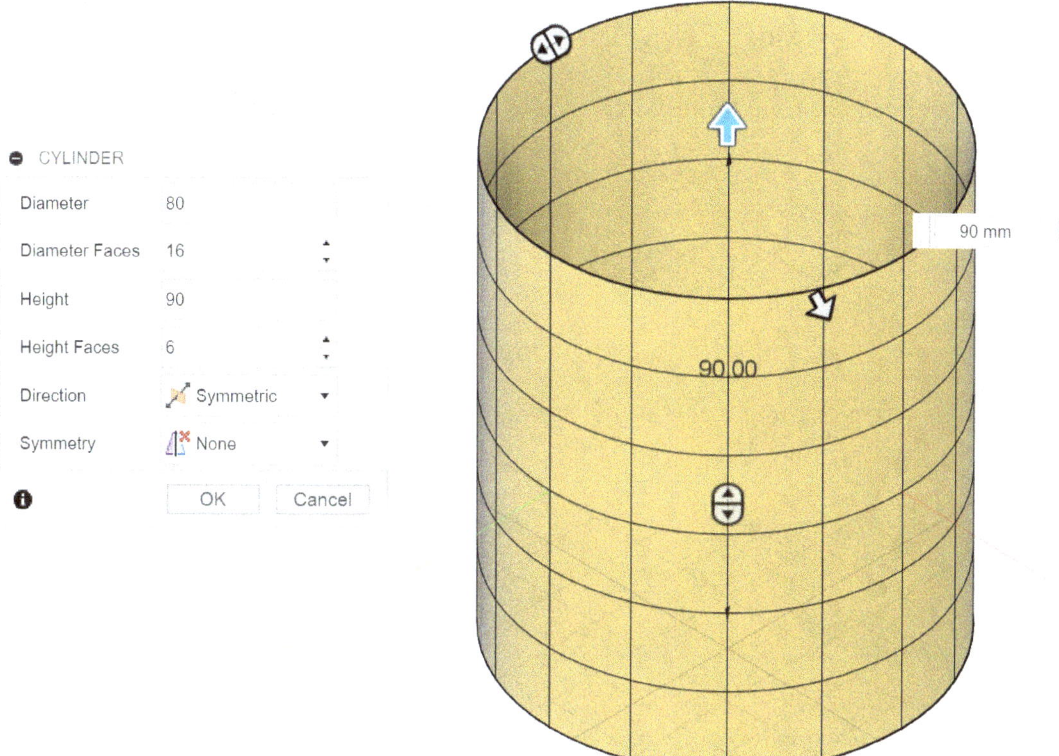

Filling the bottom Hole

1. Click the bottom right corner of the ViewCube to display the bottom portion of the cylinder.

2. Double-click on the bottom edge of the cylinder; the entire edge loop is selected.

3. On the toolbar, click **Form > Modify > Fill Hole** . On the **Fill Hole** dialog, select **Fill Hole Mode > Collapse** and click **OK**.

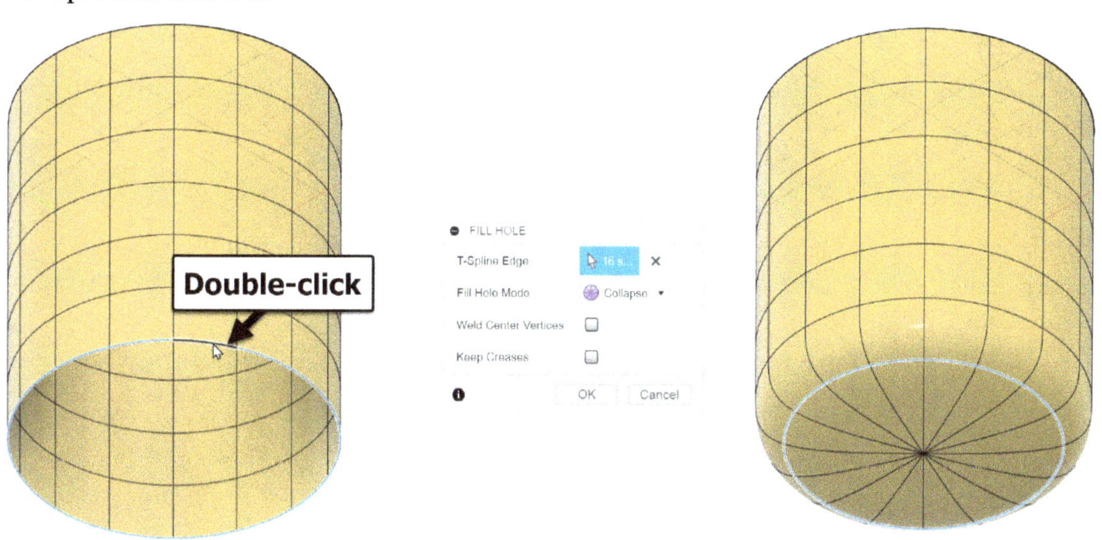

Scaling the Bottom Face

1. Press and hold the Ctrl key and select the faces at the bottom of the cylinder, as shown.
2. On the toolbar, click **Form > Modify > Edit Form**. Next, expand the **Selection Options** section on the **Edit Form** dialog and click the **Range Selection** icon; all of the faces located between the selected faces are also selected.
3. On the **Edit Form** dialog, select **Transform Mode > Scale**. Next, click and drag the corner of the XY plane of the Scale manipulator.
4. Type **0.9** in the **Scale Plane XY** box and click **OK**.

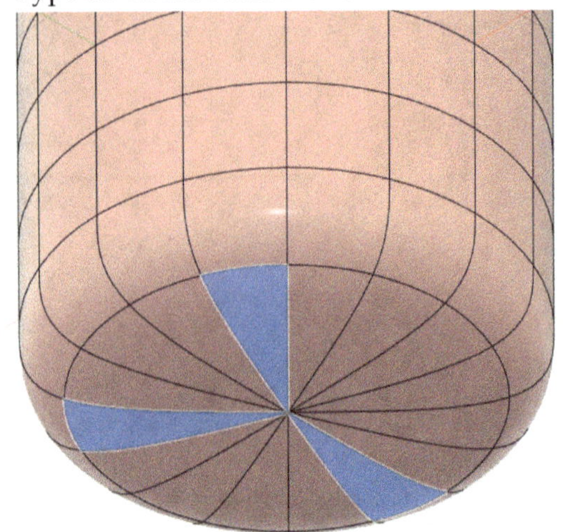
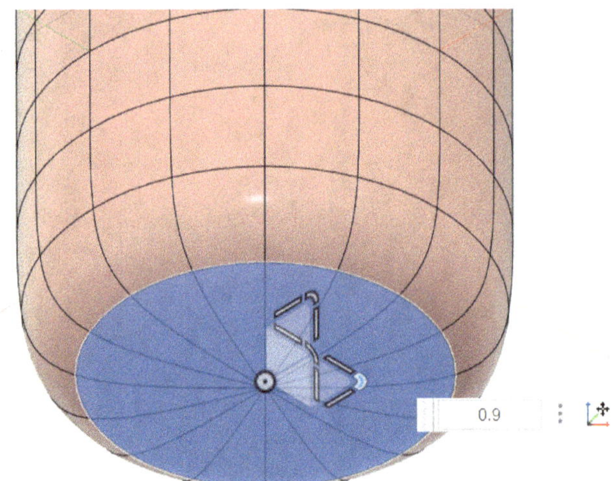

5. On the toolbar, click **Form > Create > Extrude**. Next, type **-2** and **1** in the **Distance** and **Front Faces** boxes, respectively. Next, check the **Keep Creases** option and click **OK** on the **Extrude** dialog.

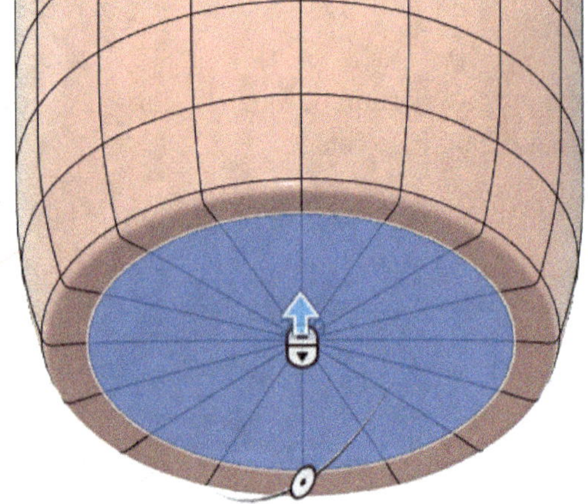
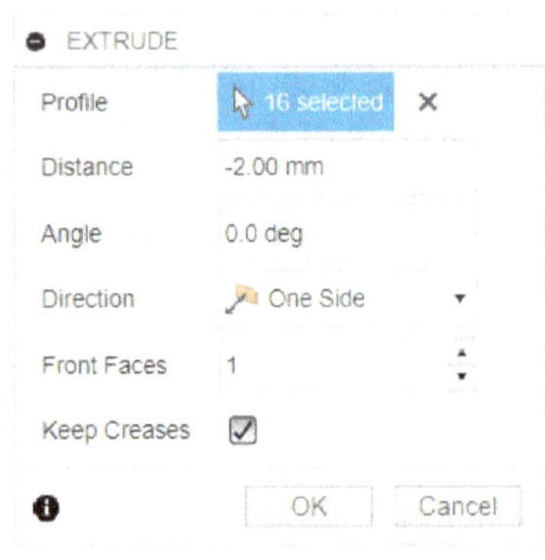

6. Double-click on the top circular edge of the cylinder. Next, click **Form > Modify > Edit Form** on the toolbar.
7. On the **Edit Form** dialog, select **Transform Mode > Scale**. Next, click and drag the corner of the XY plane of the Scale manipulator.
8. Type **1.1** in the **Scale Plane XY** box and click **OK**.

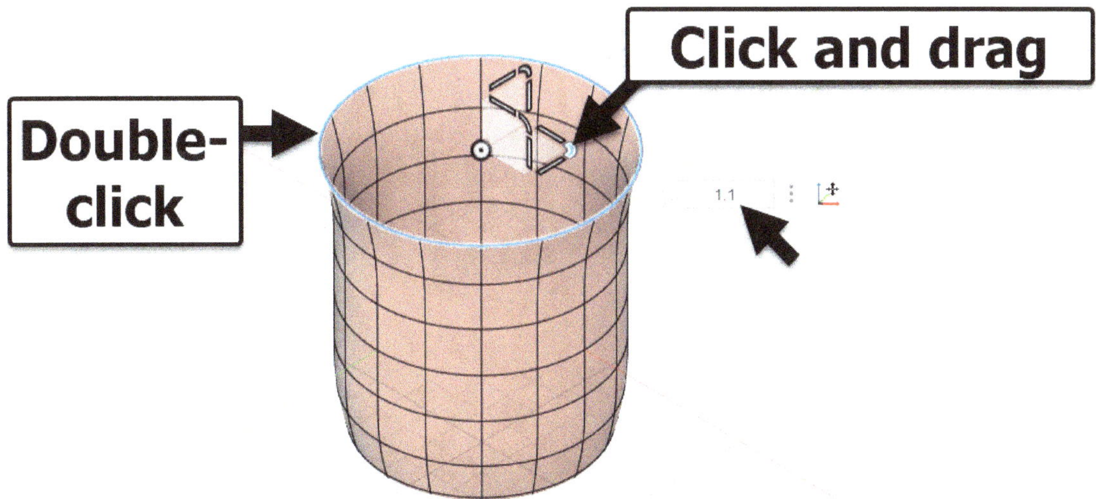

Thickening the Cylinder

1. On the toolbar, click **Form > Modify > Thicken** . Next, select the cylindrical T-spline body.
2. On the **Thicken** dialog, select **Thicken Type > Soft**. Next, select **Direction > Normal**.
3. Type **-5** in the **Thickness** box and click **OK**.

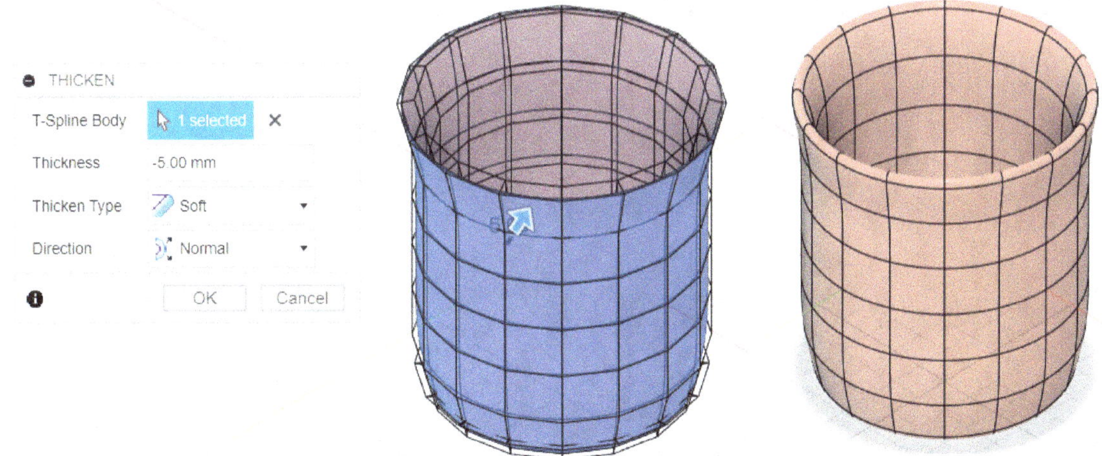

Creating the Handle

1. Click the Right face of the ViewCube; the view orientation is changed to right.
2. On the toolbar, click **Form > Modify > Bevel Edge**. Next, select the two edges a the center of the cylinder, as shown.
3. On the **Bevel Edge** dialog, type **0.5** and **1** in the **Bevel Location** and **Segments** boxes, respectively.
4. Click **OK**.

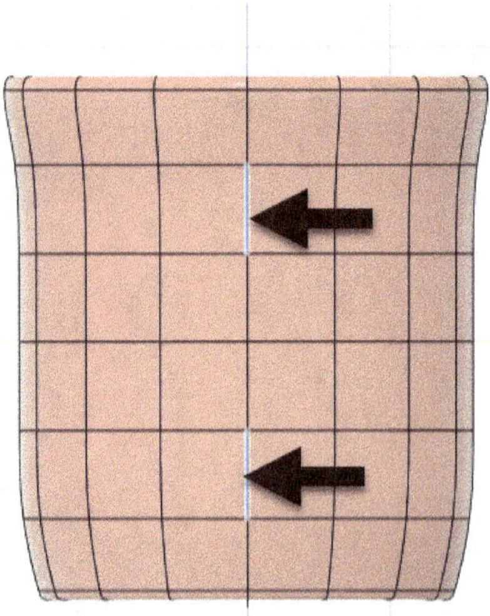 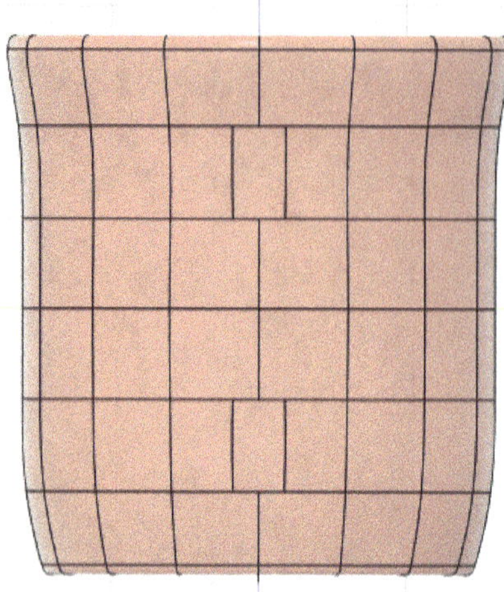

5. Click the **Home** icon located on the top right corner to change the view orientation to Isometric.
6. On the toolbar, click **Form > Create > Extrude**. Next, select the newly added faces from the T-spline body.
7. Click and drag the arrow displayed on the T-spline body toward right.
8. On the **Extrude** dialog, type **30** and **2** in the **Distance** and **Front Faces** boxes, respectively.
9. Type -10 in the Angle box and click **OK**.

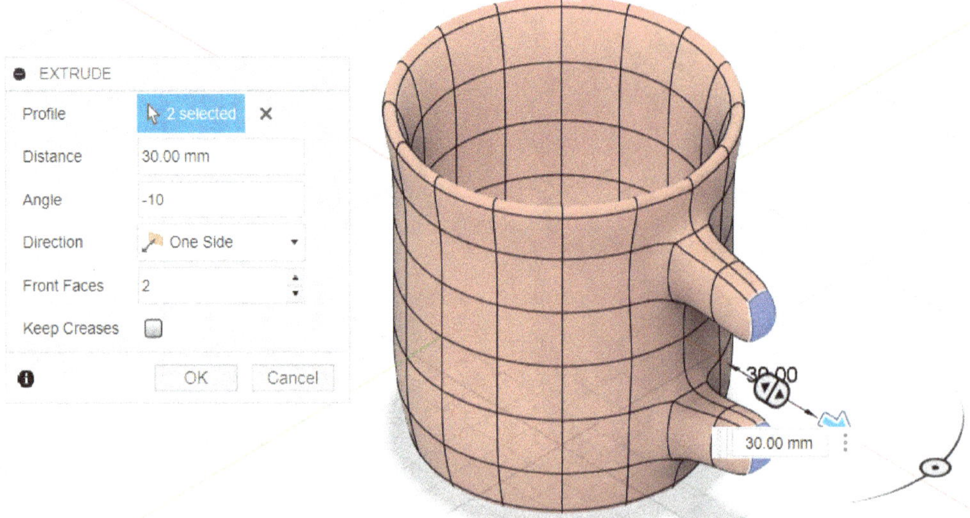

10. On the toolbar, click **Form > Modify > Bridge**. Next, select the inner faces of the lower extrusion, as shown.
11. Click the **Side 2** button on the Bridge dialog and select the inner faces of the upper extrusion, as shown.
12. Type 2 in the Faces box. Next, make sure that the arrows on the selected faces point in the same direction (Use the **Flip Side 1** and **Flip Side 2** button to change the direction the arrows displayed on the selected faces).
13. Click **OK** to bridge the selected faces.

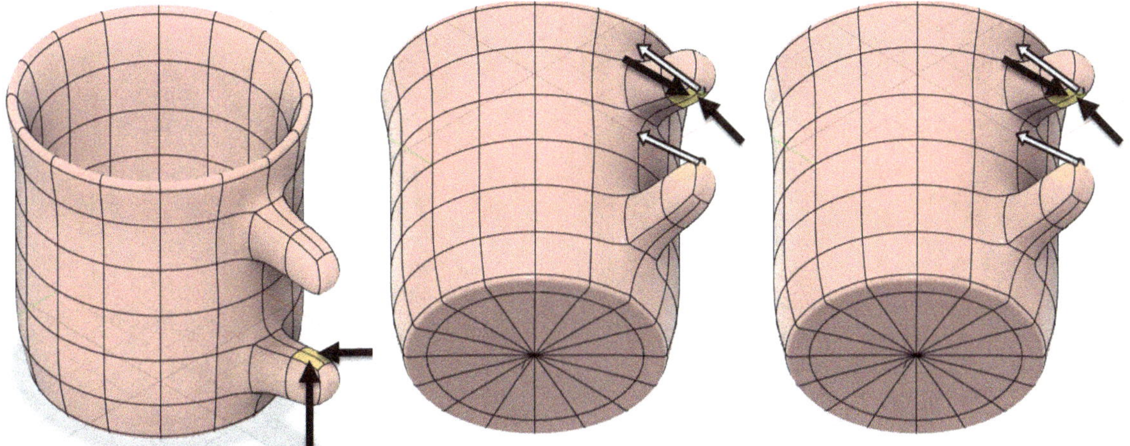

14. Click on the Front Face of the ViewCube to change the view orientation to front.

15. Click and drag a selection window from right to left across the top-right corner faces of the bridge; the faces are selected. Next, press DELETE to delete the selected faces.

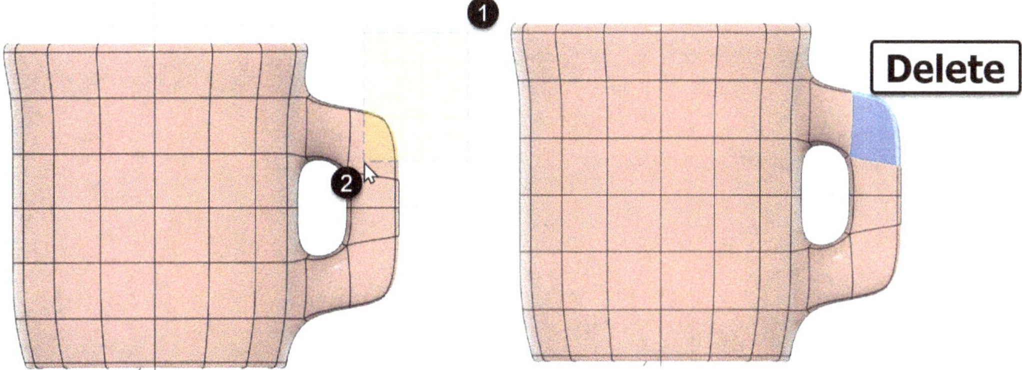

16. Click and drag a selection window from right to left across the bottom-right corner faces of the bridge. Next, press DELETE to delete the selected faces.

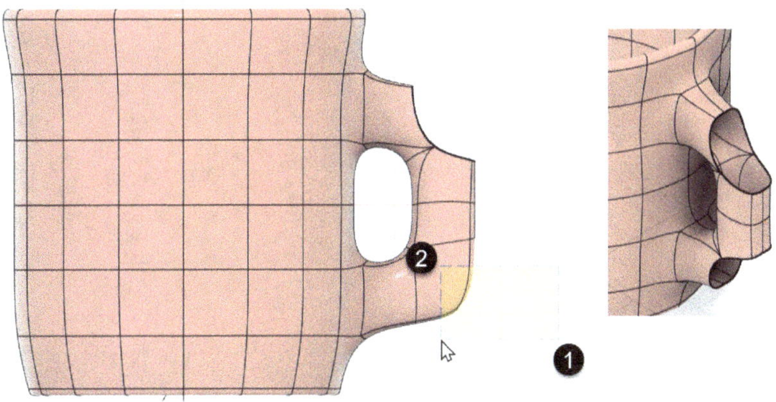

17. On the toolbar, click **Form > Modify > Merge Edge** .

18. Select the two edges of the openings created, as shown. Next, click the **Edges Group Two** Select button and select the two edges of the opening, as shown.

19. Click **OK** to merge the selected edges.

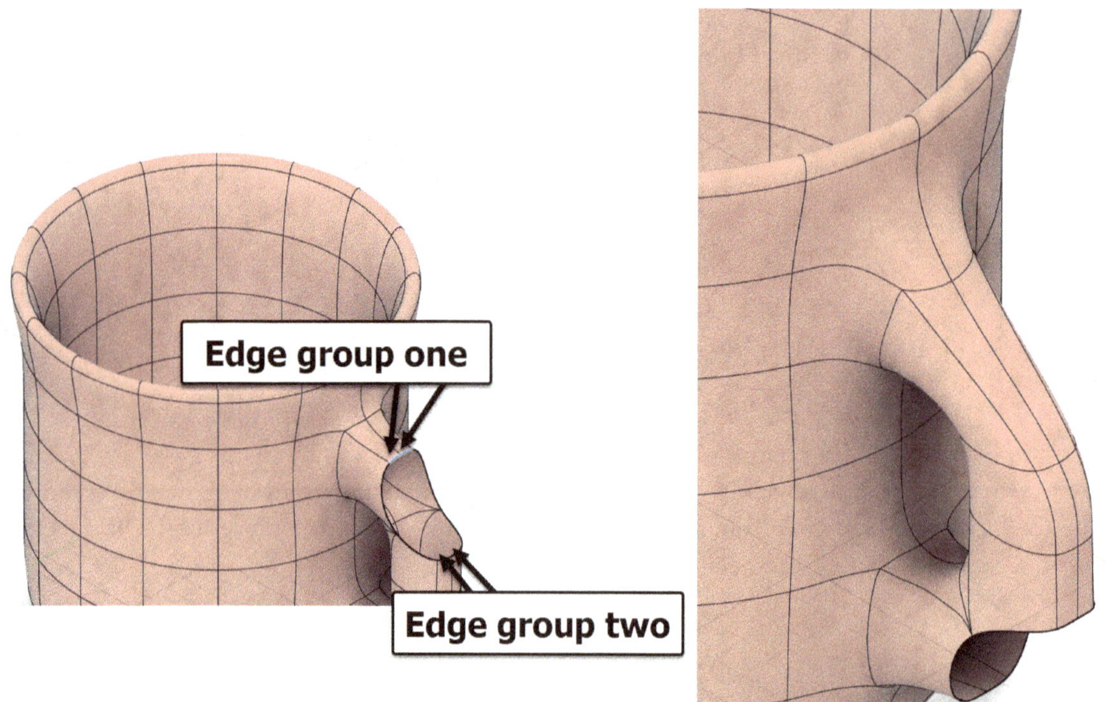

20. Likewise, merge edges on the bottom side.

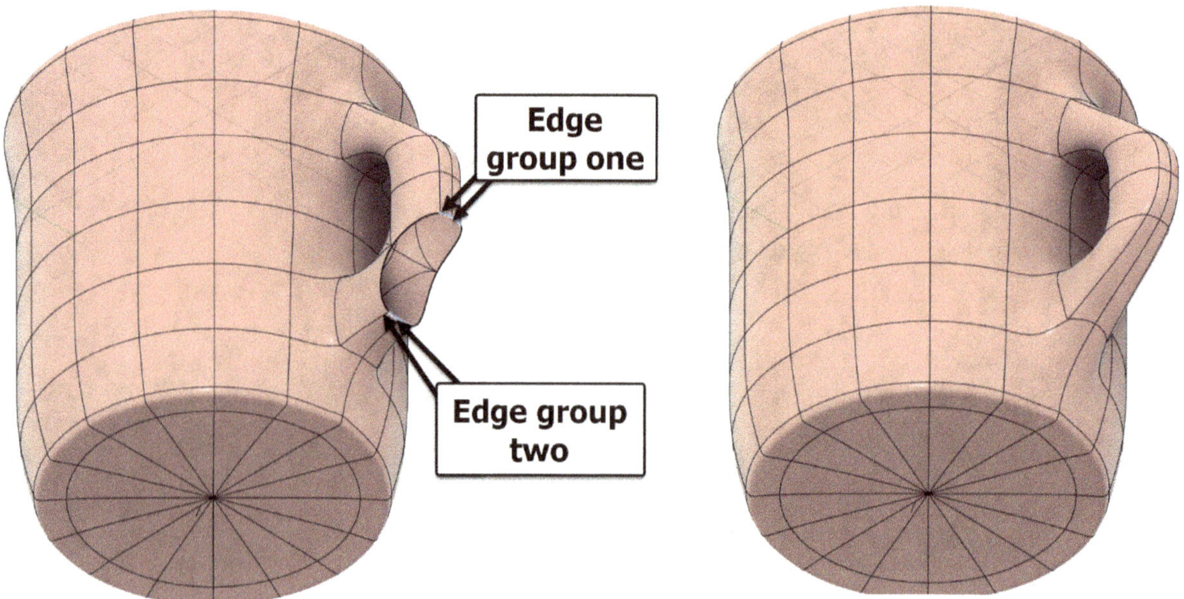

21. Click the front face of the ViewCube. Next, click and drag a selection window from right to left across the cup handle.
22. Click **Form > Modify > Edit Form** on the toolbar.
23. On the **Edit Form** dialog, click **Transform Mode > Scale**. Click and drag the top edge of the scale manipulator.
24. Type 1.2 in the Scale box.

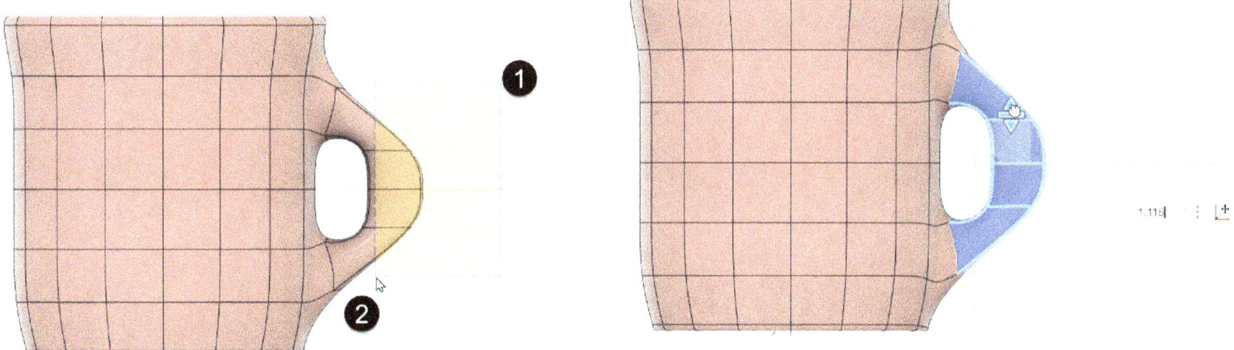

25. Click and drag the vertical edge of the Scale manipulator inward. The handle is narrowed. Click in the graphics window to deselect the handle.

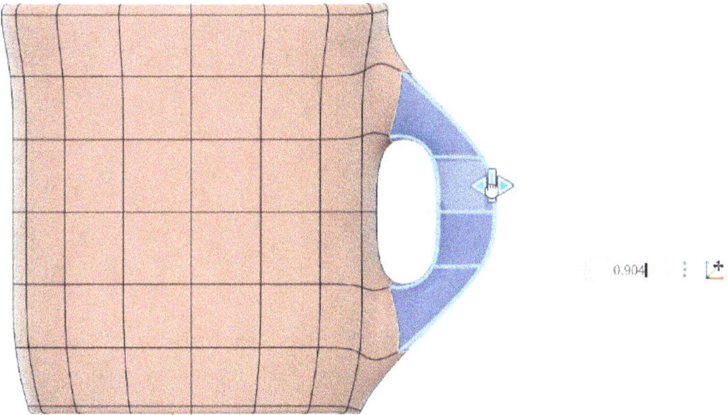

26. Click and drag a selection window across the vertical portion of the handle from the right to left.
27. Click and drag the top edge of the scale manipulator; the vertical portion of the handle is elongated.

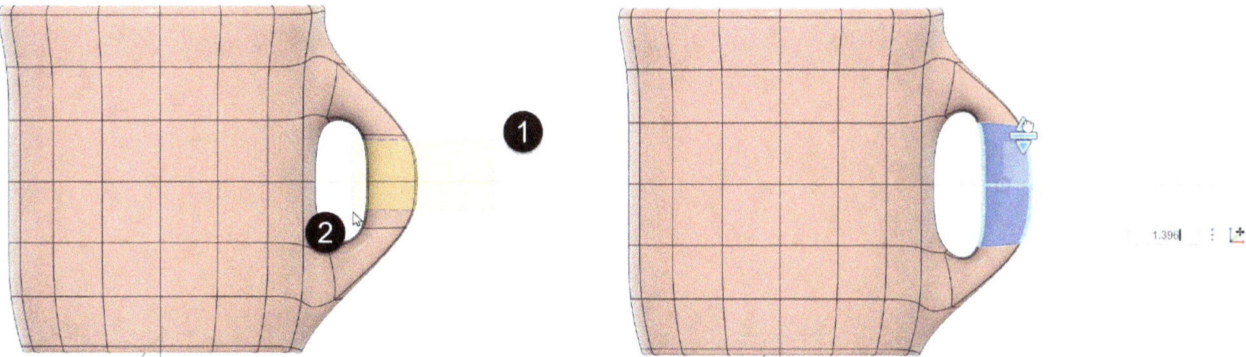

28. Click **OK** on the **Edit Form** dialog.
29. On the toolbar, click **Form > Finish Form**.
30. Save and close the part file.

Example 2

In this example, you will construct the part shown below.

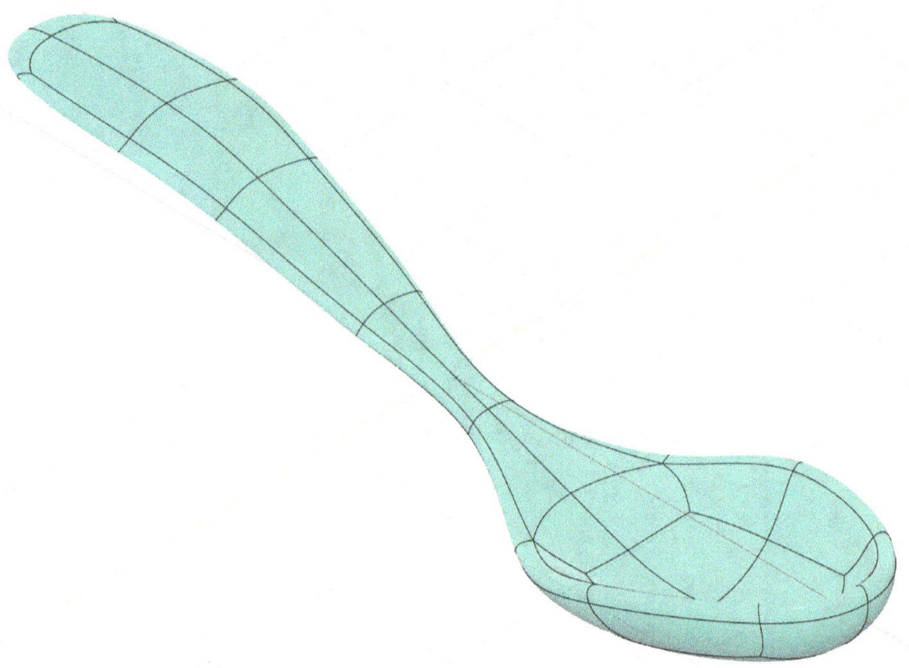

Importing the Raster Image

1. Download the image files by sending us an email to online.books999@gmail.com
2. Start **Autodesk Fusion 360.**

3. On the toolbar, click **Solid > Insert >Canvas** . Click the **Insert from my Computer** button on the **Insert** dialog.
4. Browse to the location of the downloaded files and select the Top.jpg file. Next, click the Open button.
5. Select the XY Plane from the graphics window.
6. Click the **Horizontal Flip** icon. Next, click the **Display Through** option and **OK** to insert the image file.

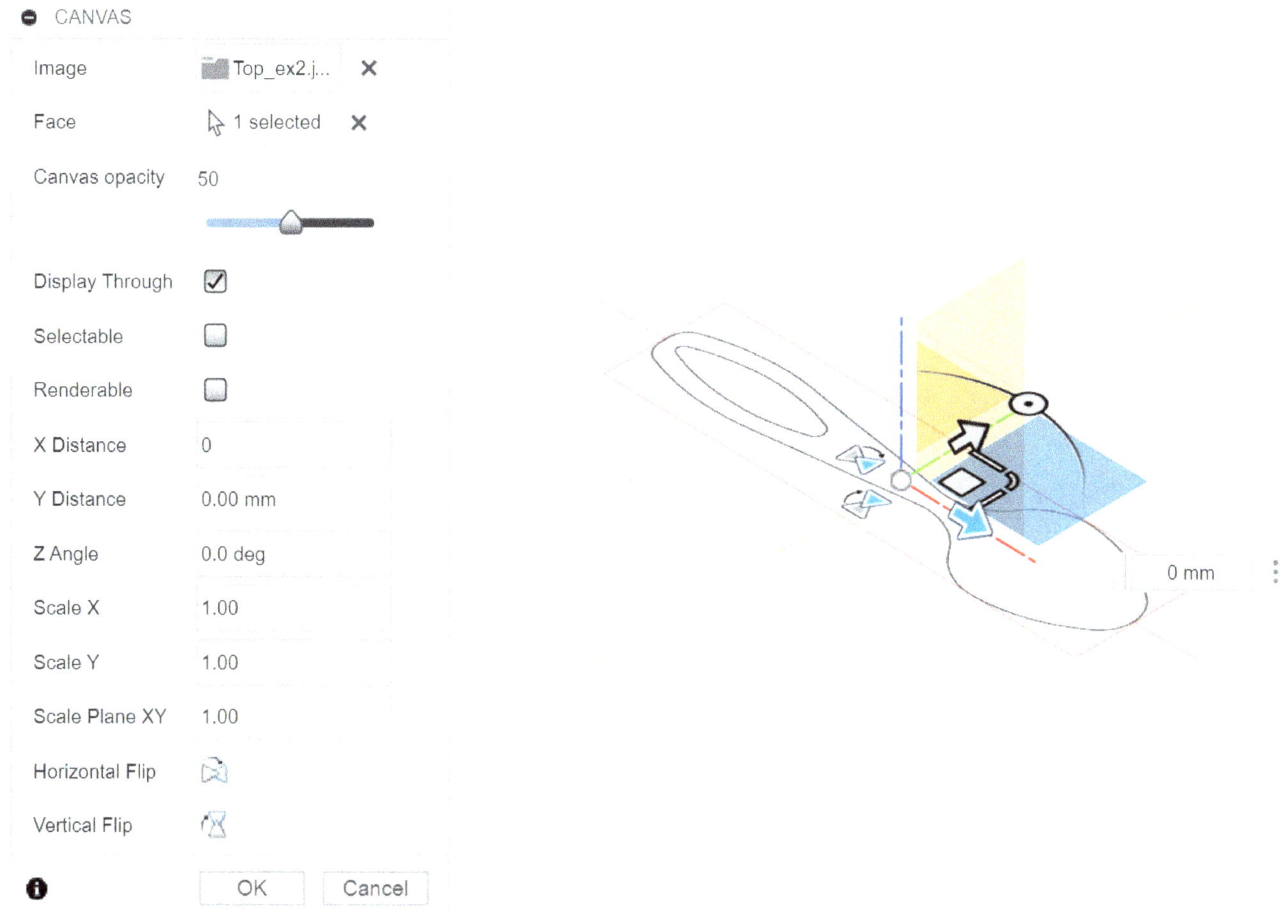

7. Likewise, insert the Front_view.jpg file on the XZ Plane.

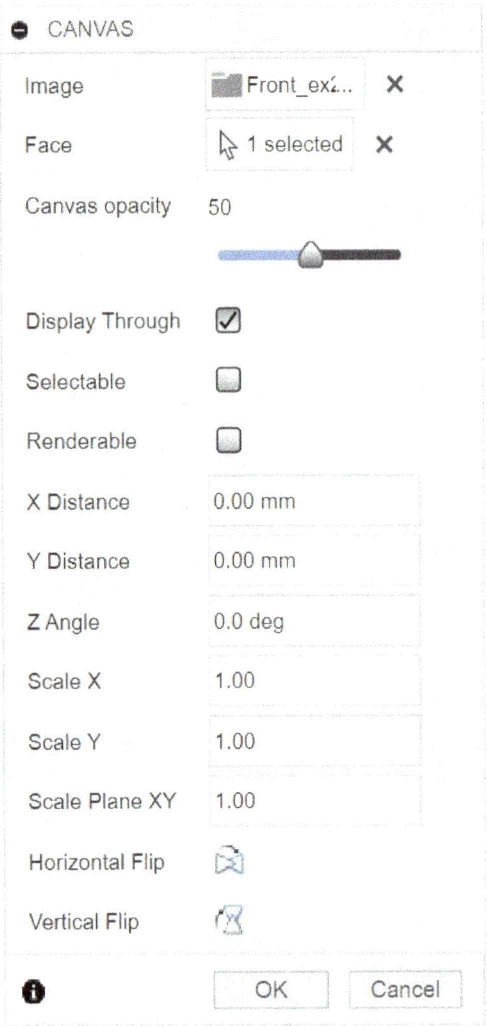

CANVAS		
Image	Front_ex2...	✕
Face	1 selected	✕
Canvas opacity	50	
Display Through	☑	
Selectable	☐	
Renderable	☐	
X Distance	0.00 mm	
Y Distance	0.00 mm	
Z Angle	0.0 deg	
Scale X	1.00	
Scale Y	1.00	
Scale Plane XY	1.00	
Horizontal Flip		
Vertical Flip		
	OK	Cancel

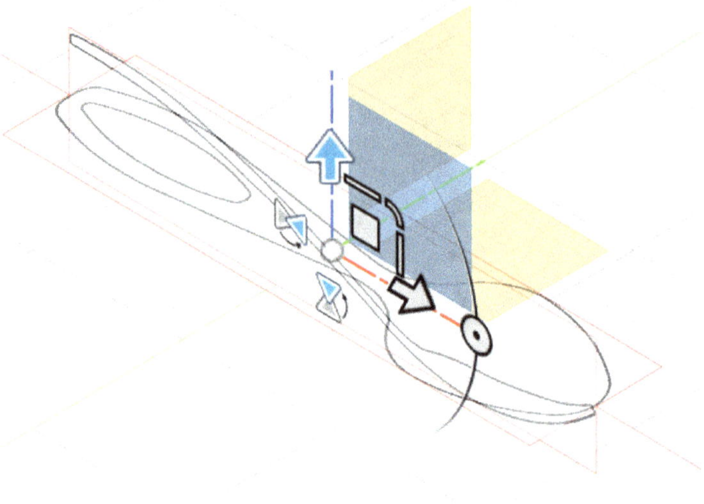

Creating and Manipulating the Quadball

1. On the toolbar, click **Solid > Create > Create Form**.
2. On the toolbar, click **Form > Create > Quadball**. Select the XY Plane from the graphics window.
3. Click the Top face of the ViewCube.
4. Specify the centerpoint of the quadball, as shown. Next, click and drag the arrow displayed to change the size of the quadball. Make sure that it fits inside the curved edges of the image.
5. Specify the options on the Quadball dialog, as shown. Click **OK** to create the quadball.

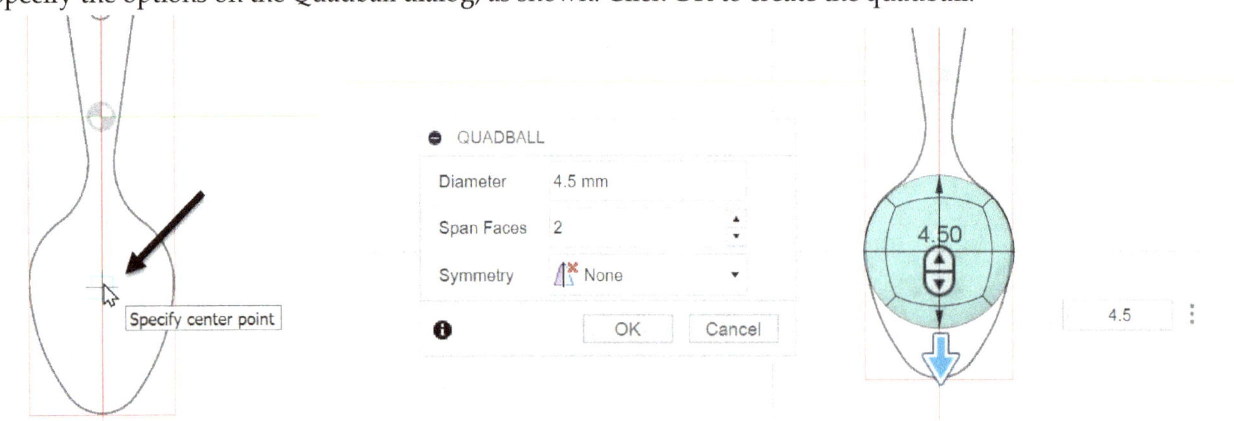

6. Create a selection window from right to left on the bottom portion of the quadball, as shown.
7. On the toolbar, click **Form > Modify > Edit Form**. Click and drag the arrow pointing downwards up to the image outline, as shown.

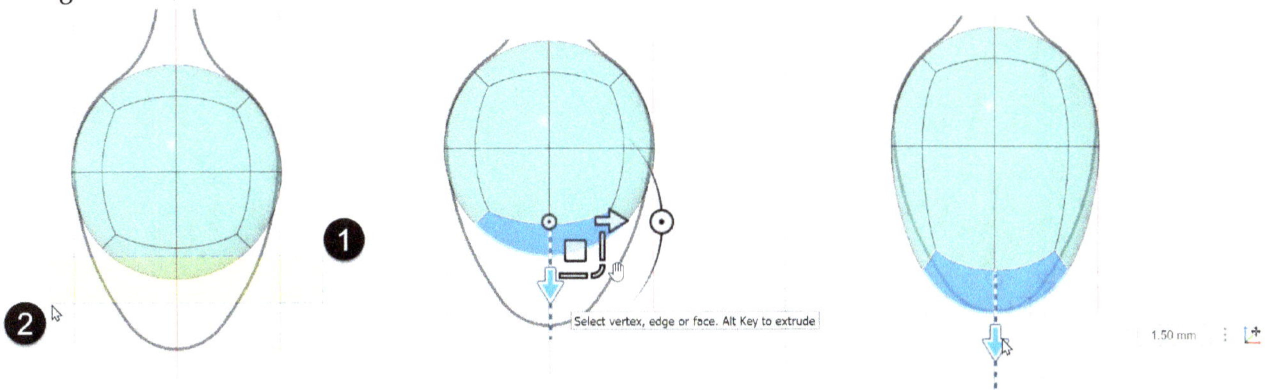

8. Click the corner fillet of the Scale manipulator such that the selected faces fit inside the image outline.

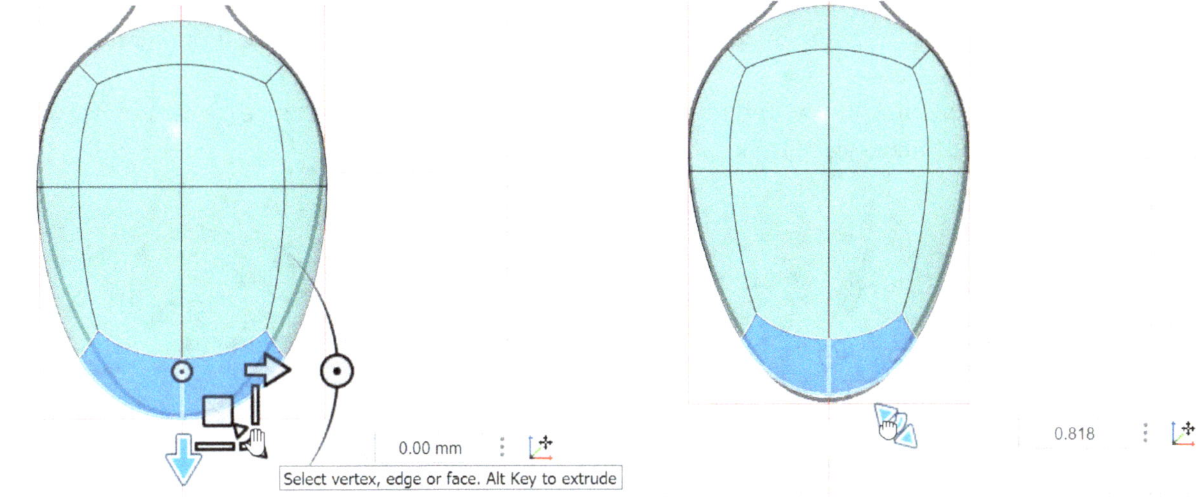

9. Click the Home icon next to the ViewCube. Next, click the Right face of the ViewCube to change the view orientation to right.
10. Create a selection window from right to left across the top portion of the quadball. Next, press Delete on your keyboard to delete the top portion of the quadball.

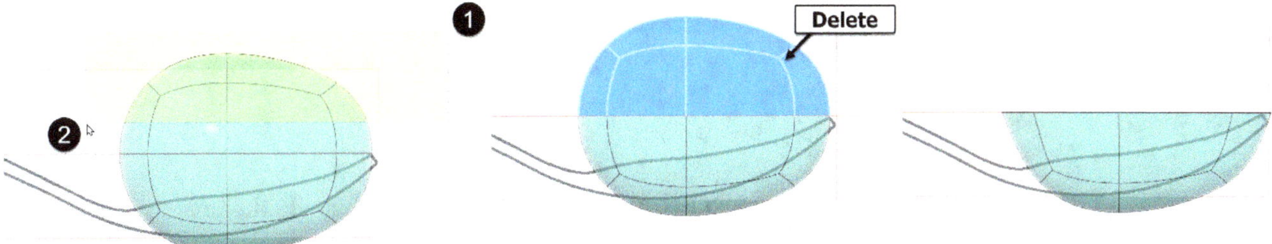

11. Create a selection window from left to right across the entire T-spline body.
12. Click **Form > Modify > Edit Form** on the toolbar. Next, click and drag the horizontal Angle handle of the manipulator in the upward direction.

13. Release the mouse pointer when the Angle value is displayed as -10. Next, click in the graphics window to deselect the T-spline body.

14. Create a selection window from right to left across the bottom faces of the T-spline body.
15. Click **Coordinate Space > Selection Space** on the **Edit Form** dialog; the manipulator is orientation in the direction of the selected faces.
16. Click the downward pointing arrow, and then drag the mouse pointer upward. Release the pointer when the selected faces are inside the image outline.

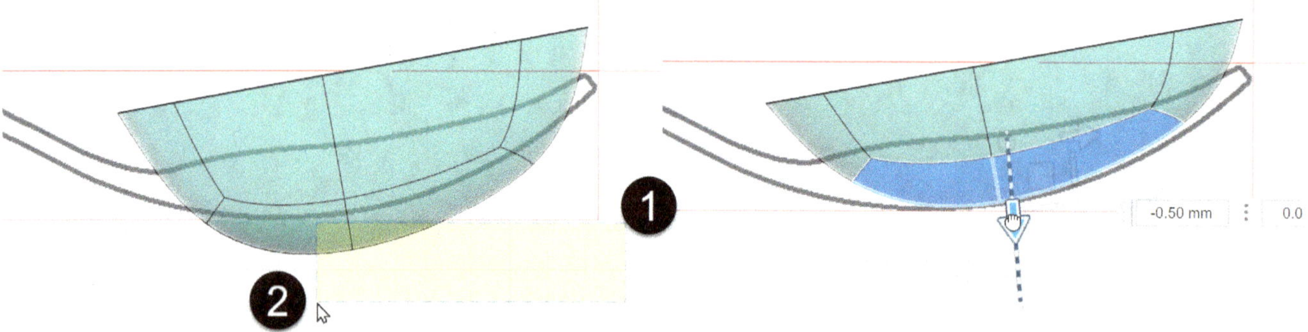

17. Create a selection window from right to left across the right face of the T-spline body.

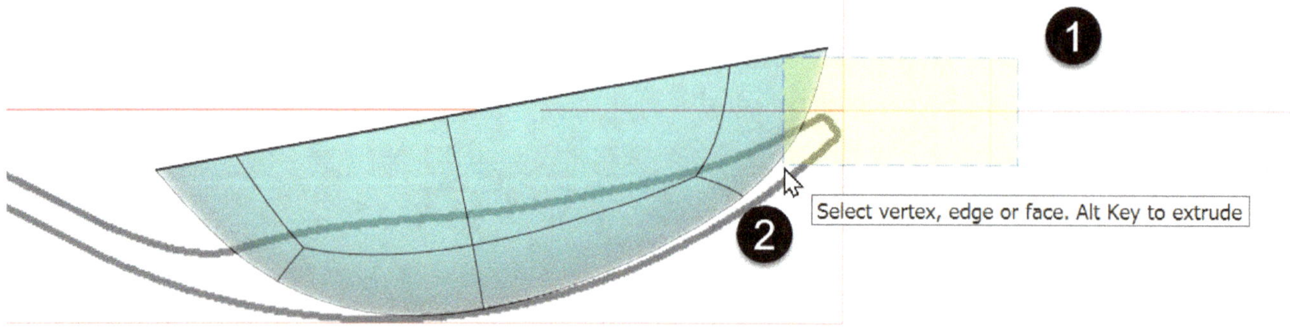

18. Click and drag the plane of the manipulator such that the T-spline body is fitted inside the image.

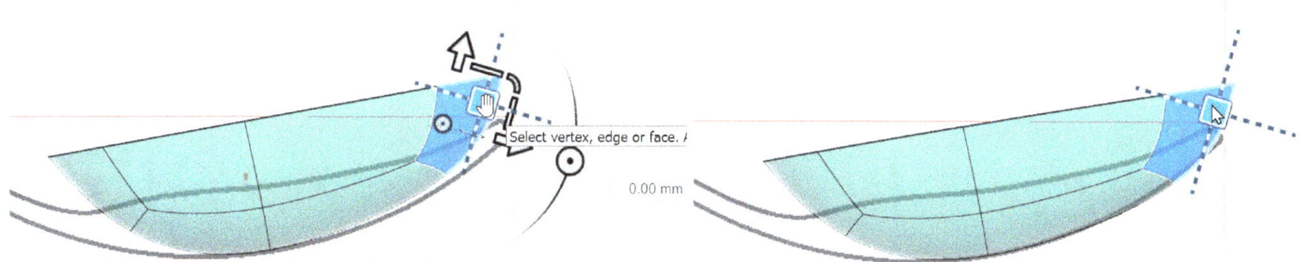

19. Click **OK** on the **Edit Form** dialog.

Creating the Handle

1. On the toolbar, click **Form > Modify > Thicken** 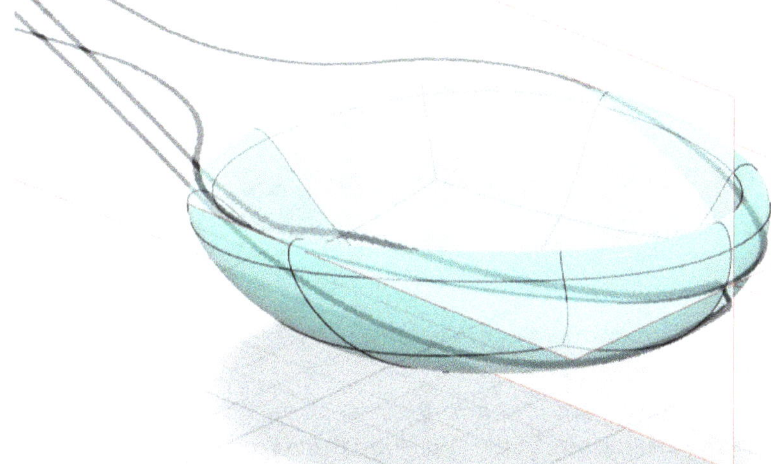. Next, select the T-spline body.
2. On the **Thicken** dialog, select **Thicken Type > Soft**. Next, select **Direction > Normal**.
3. Type **-0.5** in the **Thickness** box and click **OK**.

4. Click the top-left corner of the ViewCube to change the orientation of the model.
5. Press and hold the CTRL key and select the two faces of the T-spline, as shown.
6. Click **Form > Modify > Edit Form** on the toolbar. Next, press and hold the ALT key, click and drag the arrow pointing in the X-axis.
7. Drag the pointer up to a small distance and release the pointer.

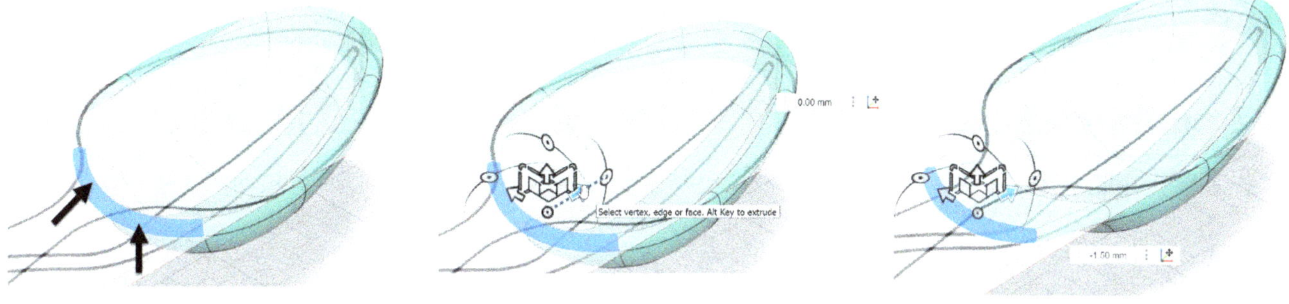

8. Again, press and hold the ALT key and drag the arrow pointing in the X-direction. Release the mouse pointer to extrude the faces.

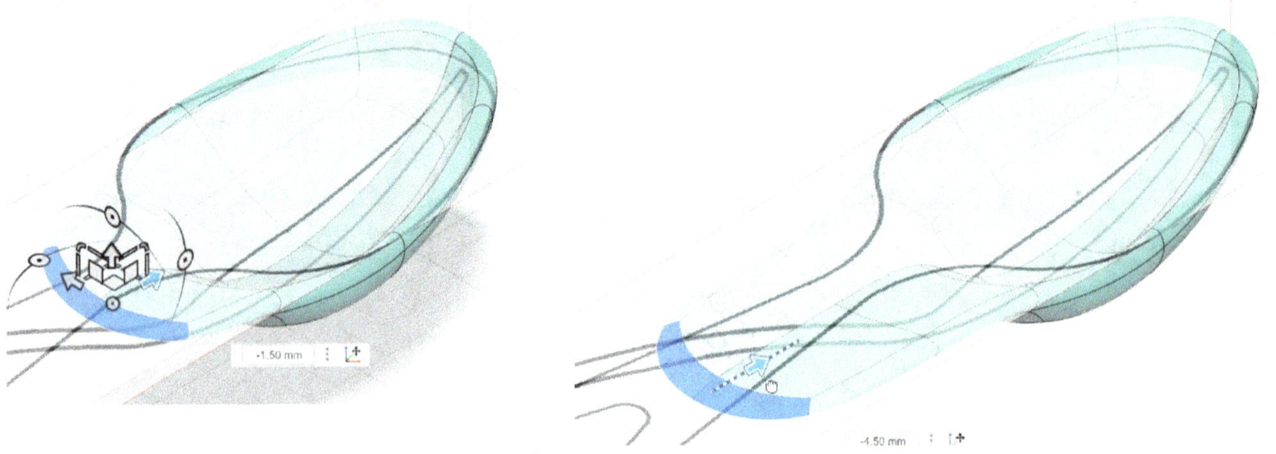

9. Likewise, create two more extrusions, as shown.

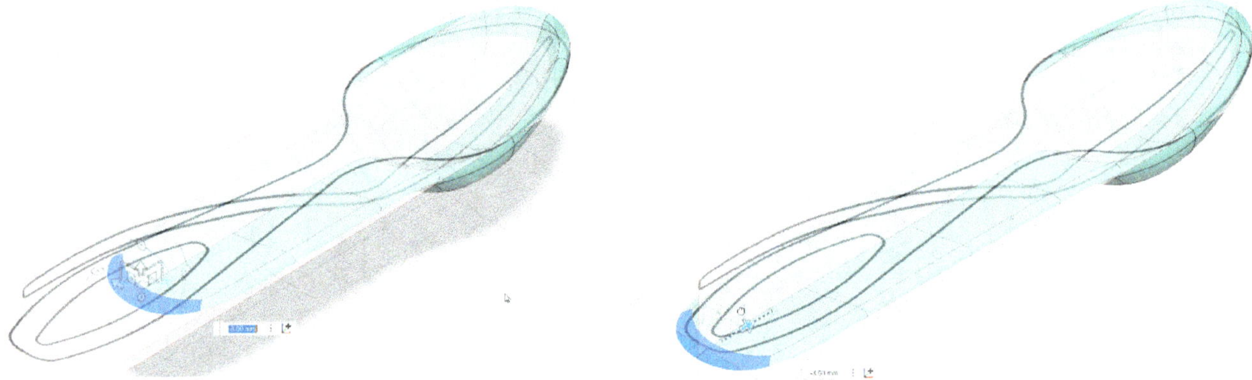

10. Click the Top face of the ViewCube to change the view orientation to Top.
11. Click in the graphics window to deselect the selected faces.
12. Double-click on the edge, as shown. The entire edge loop is selected.
13. Click on the Scale manipulator and drag it inwards; the size of the edge loop is reduced.

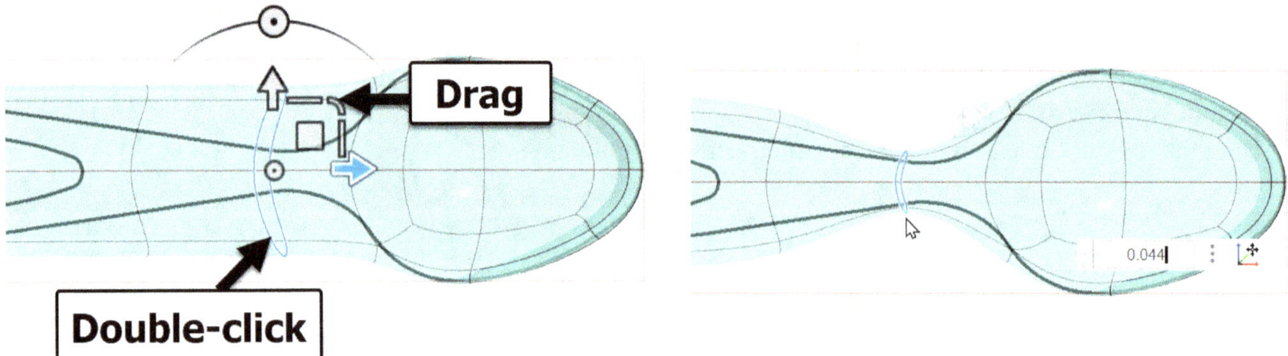

14. Click and drag the arrow pointing toward right. Move the pointer up to a small distance and release it.

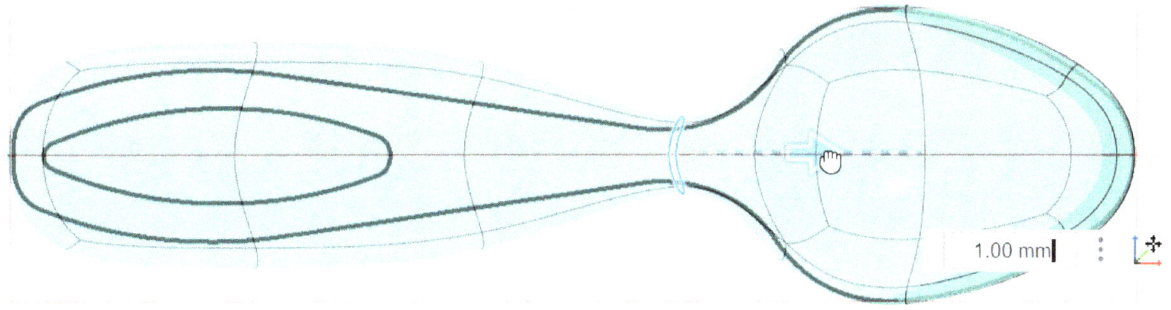

15. Double-click on the edge, as shown. Next, drag the scale manipulator to reduce the size of the selected edge loop.

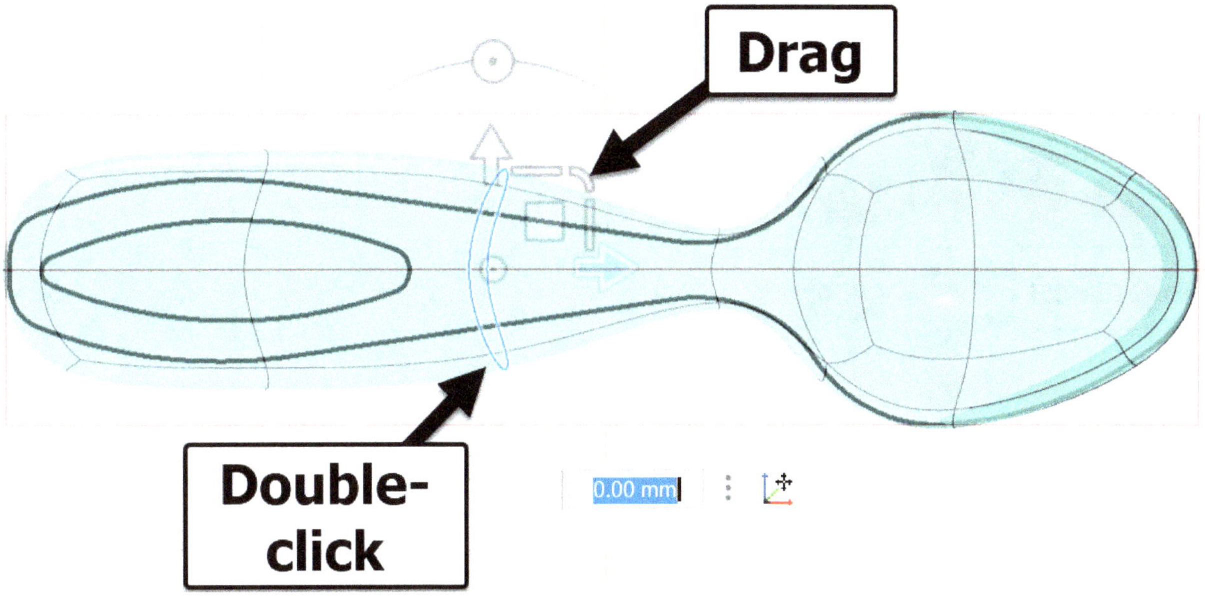

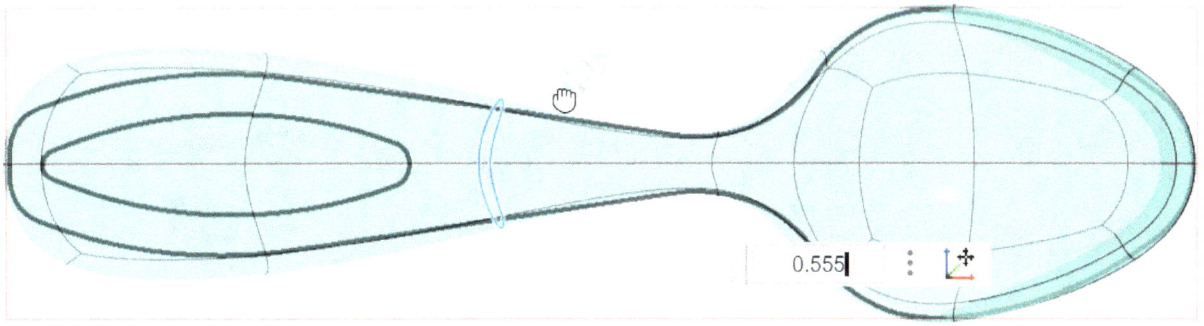

16. Likewise, the reduce the size of the edge loop, as shown.

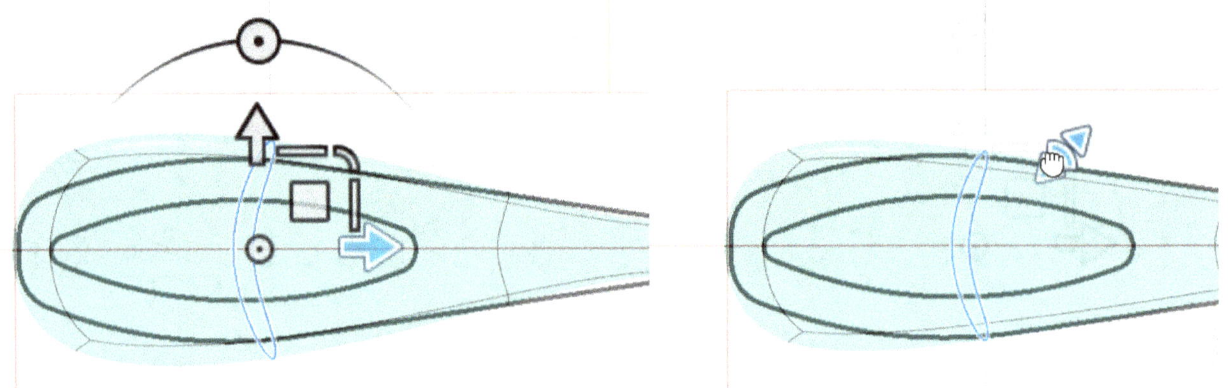

17. Click in the graphics window to deselect the selected edges.
18. Press and hold the CTRL key and select the two end faces on the left side.
19. Click and drag the Scale manipulator inwards; the selected faces are reduced in size.

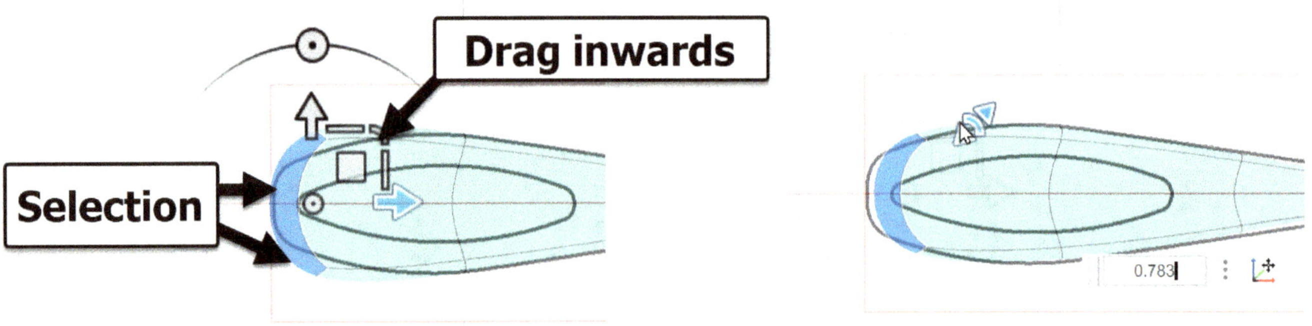

20. Click and drag the horizontal arrow toward left. Release the pointer when the T-spline body fills the image outline.

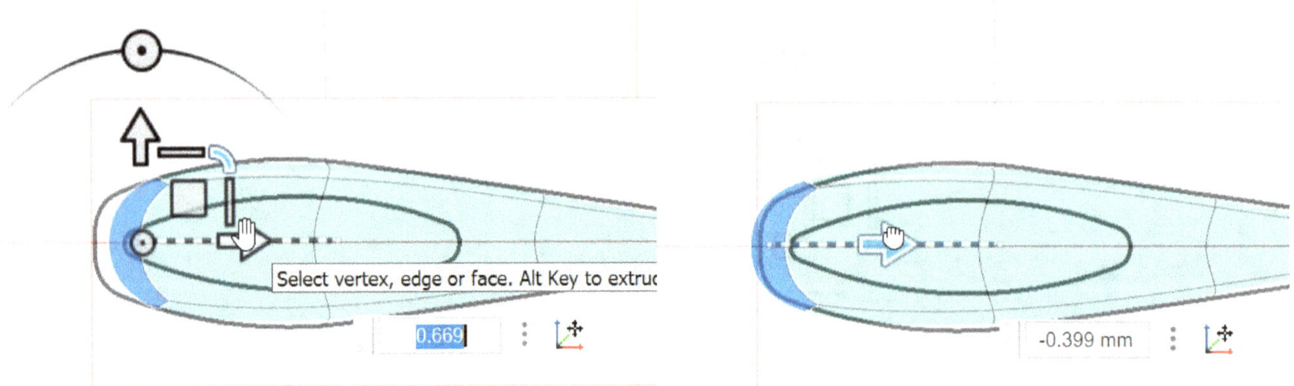

21. Change the view orientation to Front. Next, create a selection window across the narrow portion of the handle from right to left, as shown.
22. On the toolbar, click **Form > Modify > Edit Form.** Next, click and drag the vertical arrow of the manipulator in the downward direction.

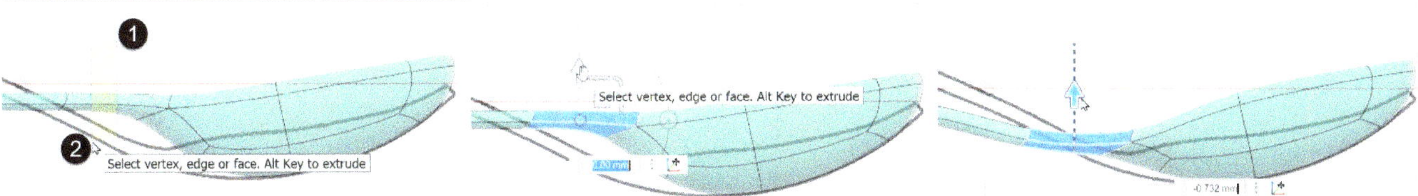

23. Click in the graphics window. Next, create a selection window from right to left across the middle portion of the spoon handle, as shown.
24. Click and drag the vertical arrow of the manipulator in the upward direction.

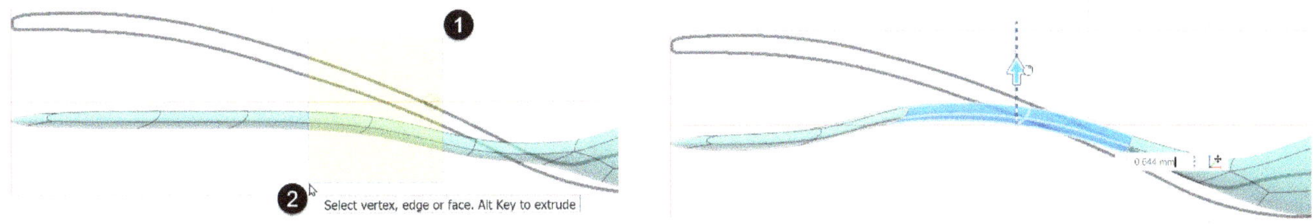

25. Click in the graphics window. Next, create a selection window from right to left across the last three faces of the spoon handle, as shown.
26. Click and drag the vertical arrow of the manipulator in the upward direction.

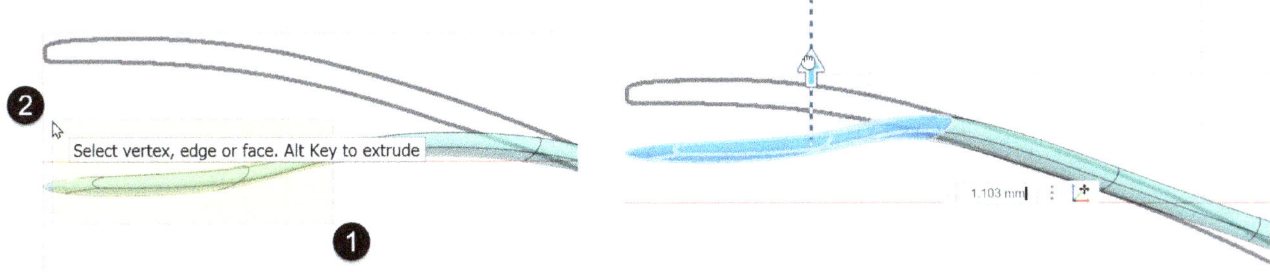

27. Click in the graphics window. Next, create a selection window from right to left across the last two faces of the spoon handle, as shown.
28. Click and drag the vertical arrow of the manipulator in the upward direction.

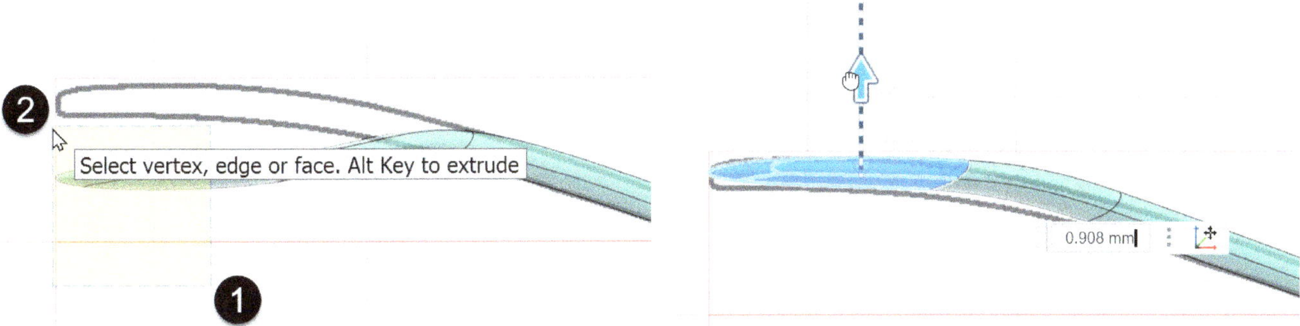

29. In the Browser, click the **Hide** icon next to the **Canvases** node; the canvas images are hidden.

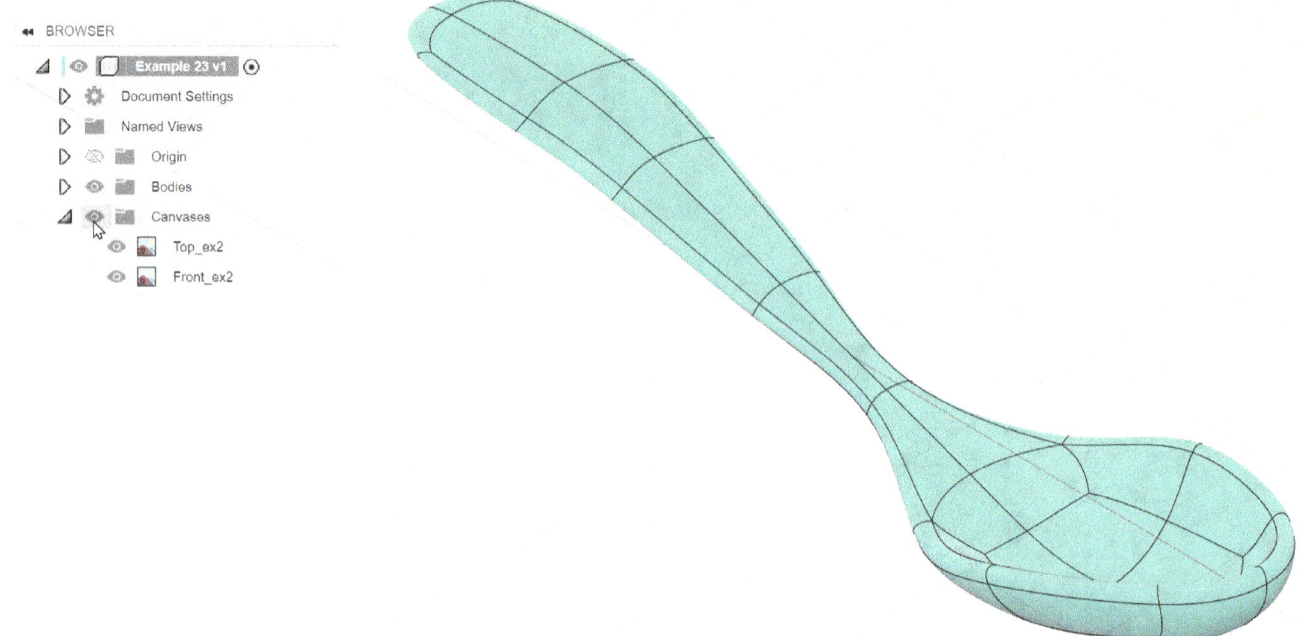

30. Save and close the file.

Questions

1. What are primitive shapes that you can create in Freeform Modeling?
2. How can you change the size of a face using the **Edit Form** command?
3. What is the difference between the **Insert Edge** and the **Subdivide** command?